Samuel French Acting

Torch Song

by Harvey Fierstein

SAMUELFRENCH.COM SAMUELFRENCH.CO.UK

FOR PRODUCTION ENQUIRIES

UNITED STATES AND CANADA
Info@SamuelFrench.com
1-866-598-8449

UNITED KINGDOM AND EUROPE
Plays@SamuelFrench.co.uk
020-7255-4302

Each title is subject to availability from Samuel French, depending upon country of performance. Please be aware that *TORCH SONG* may not be licensed by Samuel French in your territory. Professional and amateur producers should contact the nearest Samuel French office or licensing partner to verify availability.

MUSIC USE NOTE

Licensees are solely responsible for obtaining formal written permission from copyright owners to use copyrighted music in the performance of this play and are strongly cautioned to do so. If no such permission is obtained by the licensee, then the licensee must use only original music that the licensee owns and controls. Licensees are solely responsible and liable for all music clearances and shall indemnify the copyright owners of the play(s) and their licensing agent, Samuel French, against any costs, expenses, losses and liabilities arising from the use of music by licensees. Please contact the appropriate music licensing authority in your territory for the rights to any incidental music.

IMPORTANT BILLING AND CREDIT REQUIREMENTS

If you have obtained performance rights to this title, please refer to your licensing agreement for important billing and credit requirements.

TORCH SONG was initially produced by Second Stage Theater in New York in October 2017, and then in November 2018 at the Helen Hayes Theater on Broadway by Richie Jackson, Eric Kuhn & Justin Mikita, Stephanie P. McClelland, Ken Fakler, David Mirvish, Lassen Blume/ Karmen Boyz Productions, CJC & Priest/Judith Ann Abrams, Burnt Umber/True Love Productions, Caiola Productions/Torchbearers and Jujamcyn Theaters, and Second Stage Theater. The performance was directed by Moisés Kaufman, with scenic design by David Zinn, costume design by Clint Ramos, lighting design by David Lander, and projection design by John Narun. The production stage manager was Frank Lombardi. The cast was as follows:

ARNOLD . . . . Michael Urie

ED . . . . .Ward Horton

LAUREL. . . . . Roxanna Hope Radja

ALAN . . . . Michael Hsu Rosen

DAVID . . . . Jack DiFalco

MRS. BECKOFF . . . . Mercedes Ruehl

CHARACTERS

The International Stud

ARNOLD

ED

Fugue in a Nursery

ARNOLD

ED

LAUREL

ALAN

Widows and Children First

ARNOLD

ED

DAVID

MA

ACT ONE

(A light box above the stage announces:)

"THE INTERNATIONAL STUD" June 1974

(An old orange Bakelite radio glows in the preset.)

(A figure draped in a long gown enters quietly and turns up the radio...)

["I See Two Lovers" performed by Helen Morgan.*]

(The figure, **ARNOLD**, *sits down in front of a makeup table with lights and mirror. He fusses quietly. He is a young man putting on a drag face...)*

(As the song ends he clicks off the radio. He poses...)

ARNOLD. Just let me finish emasculating this eye and I'll be right with you. I think my biggest problem is being young and beautiful.

(Directly to the audience.) It's my biggest problem because I have never been young and beautiful. Oh, I've been beautiful. And Lawd knows I've been young. But never the twain have met. Not so's anyone would

---

*A license to produce *Torch Song* does not include a performance license for "I See Two Lovers." The publisher and author suggest that the licensee contact ASCAP or BMI to ascertain the music publisher and contact such music publisher to license or acquire permission for performance of the song. If a license or permission is unattainable for "I See Two Lovers," the licensee may not use the song in *Torch Song* but should create an original composition in a similar style or use a similar song in the public domain. For further information, please see Music Use Note on page 3.

7

notice anyway. A shrink acquaintance of mine believes this to be the root of my attraction to a class of men most diplomatically described as old and ugly. But I think he's underestimating my wheedles. See, an ugly person who goes after a pretty person gets nothing but trouble. But a pretty person who goes after an ugly person gets at least cab fare. Now, I ain't sayin' I never fell for a handsome face but, when *"les jeux sont faits,"* give me a toad with a pot of gold and I'll give you three meals a day! 'Cause honeys, ain't no toads when the lights go down. It's either feast or famine. It's the daylight you gotta watch out for. A thing of beauty is a joy 'til sunrise!

Now, me, if I really like a guy, I automatically wake three minutes before him giving me just enough time to unsucker my pucker, reinstate my coif, and repose my repose so's his eyes up on waking see only images by Jove thus guaranteeing my breakfast if not his real phone number.

And another hint to all present presently unattached – Cross any man off your dance card who... A: Tells you all about his wonderful mother.

B: Tells you all about his wonderful shrinker.

Or C: Refuses to tell you about his wonderful mother or shrinker.

See, a guy who's got that kind of intimate is in, what I call, "a state of confession." And experience has sorely taught me that you can never be more to those guys than fodder for *their* conversation.

Not that I got anything against analysis. I don't. I think it's a great way to keep from boring your friends. But what's good for the bored is death for the bed, if you get my drift.

Oh! There's another group you gotta watch your food stamps around – The Hopeless. They break down into three major categories: Married. Just in for the weekend. And terminally ill. Those affairs are the worst. You go into them with your eyes open, knowing the limitations, accepting them maturely and then, wham bam, you're writing letters to "Dear Abby" and burning black candles at midnight. And you ask yourself, "Wha' happened?"

You wanna know "Wha' happened"? You got just what you was asking for. The person who think they's mature enough to handle an affair that's hopeless from the beginning is the same person who keeps the publishers of Gothic Romances up to their tragic endings in mink. So, who's left? I don't know. But there are some. I had one once. His name was Charlie. He was tall, handsome, rich, deaf... Everything you could want in an affair and more. The deafness was the more. He never yelled at me. All his friends was nice and quiet. I even learned me some of that sign language.

(Demonstrating.) This means cockroach. And this is fuck. And here's my favorite. It means I Love You.

And I did. But...

(Sign language again.) Not enough.

> *(Suddenly snaps to and returns to dressing.)*

For those of yis what ain't yet guessed, I am an entertainer. Or what's left of one. I go by the name Virginia Ham. Ain't that a kick in the rubber parts? You should hear some of my former handles: Kitty Litter, Bertha Venation, Bang Bang LaDesh... There are easier things in this life than being a drag queen, but I ain't got no choice. Try as I may, I just can't walk in flats.

You know what I want? The International Stud. Not the bar. The man. I want a stud. A guy who knows what he wants and ain't a'scared to go out and get it.

A guy who satisfies his every need, but don't mind if you get what you want in the bargain. Matter of fact, he aims to please.

He'd be happy to be whatever you want him to be 'cause you're happy being what he wants you to be. The more you put in, the more you get back. An honest man. The International Stud. One size fits all.

But I wouldn't want no guy that wanted me like this here. No. I need him for the rest of the time. For the other part of me. The part that's not so well protected. Oh, there's plenty that want me like this. And I take their admiration gratefully but at a distance. A drag queen's like an oil painting – You gotta stand back from it to get the full effect.

(Standing to leave.)

My how time flies when you's doin' all the talking. Who knows, maybe he's out there tonight, right?

(Making the "I Love You" sign.)

Y'know, in my life I have slept with more men than are named or numbered in the bible. Old and new testaments put together. But not once has someone said, "Arnold, I love you," that I could believe. So I ask myself, "Do you really care?" And the honest answer is, "Yes, I care. I care a great deal. But not enough."

*(**ARNOLD** exits, leaving the radio on...)*

["Mercy Mercy Me (The Ecology)" performed by Marvin Gaye.]*

*(Pinball machines and a barroom din almost drown out the music as **ED** – handsome, charming – steps backward into a spotlight and spins around as if he's stepped on someone's foot.)*

ED. I'm sorry. I was just trying to duck that pool cue. Gets pretty crowded in here on a Saturday. Your foot okay? Good.

---

*A license to produce *Torch Song* does not include a performance license for "Mercy Mercy Me (The Ecology)." The publisher and author suggest that the licensee contact ASCAP or BMI to ascertain the music publisher and contact such music publisher to license or acquire permission for performance of the song. If a license or permission is unattainable for "Mercy Mercy Me (The Ecology)," the licensee may not use the song in *Torch Song* but should create an original composition in a similar style or use a similar song in the public domain. For further information, please see Music Use Note on page 3.

(Turns away but then tries to sneak a look behind him. He gathers his courage and turns around...)

Look, the name's Ed Reiss. My friends call me Ed. I'm Sagittarius.

What's so funny?

Some people like to know that stuff. I don't believe any of it myself, but I have done some reading... See, I like to know what's expected of me.

You have a beautiful smile. No, really, you do. Can I get you another beer?

One Lite coming up.

(To bartender.) A Lite, please.

So, what's your name?

Arnold. Your friends call you Arnie or Arn?

Arnold. Nice to meet you, Arnold. So, you Italian? Spanish?

Jewish! I never would have guessed. Not with those dark romantic eyes. So, I don't remember ever seeing you here before. I don't get in that often. I teach over in Brooklyn and have to be up and out pretty early, so if I'm feeling horny this is where I come. I can be in and out of the backroom and home within an hour.

Oh. Well... I'm off tomorrow, so... You really do have beautiful eyes. Are you wearing makeup?

No. I didn't think so. So, how's the backroom? Crowded? Never?

No. It's just you don't expect to meet someone in a backroom bar who's never been in the backroom. So, you here alone?

How lucky for me. You live alone?

Well, look, I have a car. I'd ask you back to my place but I have a roommate. Straight.

He's got a thing about gays. It's his place. I sublet.

Oh, well, I date women too. I really live upstate. I own a farm about an hour south of Montreal. That's my real home.

I spend most of my weekends there and then all of the summer vacation. You'll love the house. One of those old Victorian farmhouses. Lots of gingerbread and Franklin stoves. My father is helping me restore it.

No. They winter in Florida and then come north to spend the warmer months with me. Hey, what say we continue this conversation in the car?

Great. By the way, what do you do?

I meant for a living.

You can really make a living doing that?

I've got to admit, you're my first. Has anyone ever told you you have a very sexy voice?

You really do. Is it natural or do you have a cold?

> *(Gesturing for Arnold to lead the way.)*
>
> *(Lights up on the radio.)*
>
> *["96 Tears" performed by Big Maybelle.*]*
>
> *(The guitar lick plays through the radio speaker as* **ARNOLD** *appears, sitting on a chair, staring at a silent telephone...)*
>
> *(As the song resolves,* **ARNOLD** *lifts the receiver, dials quickly, and waits impatiently for someone to answer.)*

ARNOLD. Hello, Murray? Call me back.

> *(He slams the receiver down and waits. And waits. And, finally, the phone rings...)*

Goddammit, Murray, what took you so long? The shower could have waited Murray...the shampoo in the

---

*A license to produce *Torch Song* does not include a performance license for "96 Tears." The publisher and author suggest that the licensee contact ASCAP or BMI to ascertain the music publisher and contact such music publisher to license or acquire permission for performance of the song. If a license or permission is unattainable for "96 Tears," the licensee may not use the song in *Torch Song* but should create an original composition in a similar style or use a similar song in the public domain. For further information, please see Music Use Note on page 3.

shower could have waited, Murray... The man with the shampoo in the shower could have waited, Murray. Whatever. I can't talk now. I gotta keep the line free.

(Starts to hang up...)

What?

I just wanted to make sure the phone was working.

Ed. I'm expecting a call from Ed.

When? Well, it is now Tuesday, eight p.m. Ed's gonna call sometime after Tuesday, eight p.m.

Well, of course he's going to call, Murray. You think I'd sit by the phone for six days if he wasn't going to call?

Murray, when you have been seeing someone for almost six months, you build a relationship based on trust and mutual respect. Something you and your magic fingers shower massage would not understand. He will call, Murray. He knows when he's got a good thing going. He knows I ain't like those other cheap tricks he sees. Oh, no, Murray, he will call. And when he does... And when he does... And when he does... The phone's gonna be free!

(He slams down the receiver.)

Oh, ye of little faith.

(He picks up the receiver and dials.)

*(**ED** appears in his apartment, a bottle of wine and a corkscrew in hand. He answers the phone...)*

ED. Hello?

ARNOLD. Hi. Was that you?

ED. Oh, hi. Was what me?

ARNOLD. Just now on the phone. Was that you trying to get me?

ED. Uh... No.

ARNOLD. Oh. Then I wonder who it was. See, I just walked in the door this second. You know, I've been out of town all week and I just got back and I was fumbling at the

door with my bag and the keys when I heard the phone
ringing. So, of course, I dropped the keys. And when I
bent over to pick them up I dropped the luggage and
one of the latches uncaught and everything fell out all
over the place.

So, finally I get the door open and kick everything
inside, dive at the phone and pick it up just in time to
hear whoever it was hang up.

> *(Silence.)*

So, hi.

ED. I was going to call you real soon. I've just been really
busy.

ARNOLD. What's the difference? We're talking now, right?

ED. Look, Arnold, I've got a friend coming for dinner and...

ARNOLD. That's okay. No problem. I just called 'cause I
thought it was you calling me. So, give me a call when
you're not so busy.

ED. I'm sorry. I'll call you tomorrow.

ARNOLD. Sure. Great. Fine. I understand.

ED. What do you understand? You never give me a chance
to call. Every time I'm just about to, there you are calling
me.

ARNOLD. ESP maybe. Hey, think of all the money I save
you on your phone bill.

ED. You're impossible. You know that?

ARNOLD. Yeah. It's a wonder you put up with me.

ED. So... How was your trip?

ARNOLD. My tri... Oh, my trip. Smooth. Who's coming over
for dinner.

ED. A friend. You don't know him.

ARNOLD. How do you know? I know lots of hims. "Battle
Hymn of the Republic," "O Come Emmanuel"...

ED. Impossible.

ARNOLD. So, is it an old him or a new him?

ED. A new one.

ARNOLD. Ah. And where did you meet him? The Stud?

ED. Why do you do this to yourself?

ARNOLD. What? I'm asking a question. Can't a person show a little interest in another person's life? So?

ED. I've really got to go, Arnold. I'll call you. Promise.

ARNOLD. That's what you said last week.

ED. Maybe if you gave me a chance to call...

ARNOLD. That's all I'm asking you for; a chance. Why're you treating me like some trick you picked up last night?

ED. Let me call you tomorrow...

ARNOLD. What's wrong, Ed? Until last week I could've sworn things were going great for both of us. What's happening?

ED. Not now, Arnold.

ARNOLD. Yes, now!

ED. Arnold, I'm just going to get angry.

ARNOLD. Get angry. Just talk to me.

ED. This is not going to do any good for either one of us.

ARNOLD. Who said you decide what's good and what's not? Maybe it's just what we need. Maybe it's what I need. You can't expect me to just sit around here waiting for you to call.

ED. I never asked you to. I told you to go out, have a good time, meet other people...

ARNOLD. I can't. All right? I'm not built that way.

ED. Well, I'm not ready to make a commitment.

ARNOLD. And I'm not asking you to. But if I have to accept you going out, then you have to accept that I'm not.

ED. You are crazy.

ARNOLD. I'm lonely.

ED. That's not my fault.

ARNOLD. Wanna bet?

ED. You've got no right to make me feel guilty.

ARNOLD. I happen to be in love with you. That must give me some kind of rights. And if it don't give me the right to see you then at least I got the right to bitch about it.

ED. What do you want me to say?

ARNOLD. I want you to tell me what's going on. I want you to tell me how, in two short weeks, we've gone from being together to whatever the hell you'd call this.

ED. You're being very difficult.

ARNOLD. Talk to me! Is it your parents coming north? Is that it?

ED. What if I came over straight from school tomorrow?

ARNOLD. No! I want to hear it now. I know what'll happen if you come over, everything will be great just like it always is when we're together and we'll never even mention tonight. No, I want to hear from this side of you.

ED. She's going to be here any minute... I'll come over after work. I promise. Okay?

    (Silence.)

Hello? Arnold?

ARNOLD. She? Ed, did you say, she?

ED. Shit.

ARNOLD. Oh, shit! Thank God. For a minute there I thought you said, she.

ED. I did say she. I'm seeing a woman.

ARNOLD. And you called me crazy?

ED. And this is exactly why I didn't want to discuss it on the phone.

ARNOLD. You're right. It would make much more sense if we discussed it after sex. It *is* your parents.

ED. It is not.

ARNOLD. Then why all of a sudden like this?

ED. Don't make believe I never told you about my relationships with women.

ARNOLD. Sure you told me about your women relations, but I thought you meant sisters and aunts and nieces.

ED. That's not funny.

ARNOLD. I think it's hysterical.

(Pause.)

So... How long has this been going on?

ED. Not long.

ARNOLD. How'd you meet her?

ED. My friends, Bob and Janet asked if I was seeing anyone because they had this girl they wanted me to meet.

ARNOLD. And what did you say when they asked if you were seeing anyone?

ED. I said I wasn't. Well, I could hardly tell them about you, could I?

ARNOLD. God forbid. What's she like?

ED. Why don't you call me a bastard and hang up?

ARNOLD. I want to understand. Talk to me.

ED. Well, she's wonderful.

ARNOLD. Bastard! And what did you tell her about me?

ED. Nothing.

ARNOLD. That does seem to be my name. But you told her you date guys.

ED. I didn't think it was important.

ARNOLD. Of course not.

ED. I think there are private things that should remain private.

ARNOLD. You don't think that's being just a little dishonest?

ED. No. We have a more mature relationship than that.

ARNOLD. Of course you do. So, when are you taking her to meet the folks?

ED. This weekend.

ARNOLD. I don't believe a word of this. Tell me again they have nothing to do with this sudden burst of heterosexuality. Look, Ed, I don't know much about heterosexuals, but I do know that when a guy takes a gal to meet his folks, for the weekend no less, this is no longer casual dating. Don't you think you're being unfair to her, (not to mention what you're doing to me)? Doesn't she have the right to know what she's getting herself into?

(No response.)

ARNOLD. What's the matter? Catch your tongue in the closet door?

ED. You're really dragging me over the coals.

ARNOLD. Why should I be the only one with a barbecued ass? And if I may ask another stupid question: What am I supposed to do?

ED. That's up to you.

ARNOLD. Not entirely.

ED. I want us to go on seeing each other. You may not believe this, but I really don't want to lose you.

ARNOLD. That's hitting below the belt – Appealing to my Susan Hayward fantasies. Arnold Beckoff – Back Street Woman.

ED. That's a little over the top even for you.

ARNOLD. Really? Then take me to meet your parents.

ED. I could if I wanted. They'd understand.

ARNOLD. And maybe they can explain it to you.

ED. Your kindness is appreciated.

ARNOLD. Listen, Mr. Reiss, at this moment I don't think kindness is something you should be expecting. I'm sorry. I'm sorry I just feel so helpless.

ED. You helpless?

ARNOLD. Dumb huh? I don't understand. I thought we were so happy. That we were so special. The way we made love...the way you cried in my arms... What are we doing?

ED. I don't know... I'm confused...

ARNOLD. Ed, come over.

ED. I can't. I know what I want. I'm doing what I have to do.

ARNOLD. We can just talk.

ED. I'm not like you, Arnold. I don't want to live in a ghetto of gay bars and backrooms scared that someone will find out. I could be fired. I want more. I've got to be comfortable with who I am.

ARNOLD. How can sleeping with a woman make you comfortable if you know you'd rather be with a man? How are you supposed to get respect from anyone if you won't be yourself? There's no you to respect.

ED. And where's your self-respect? Huh? I certainly don't see any here.

ARNOLD. You wanna see my self-respect? Here! Here's my self-respect.

(**ARNOLD** *slams the receiver down on its cradle.*)

(*The lights black out on* **ED**.)

(*Moment of realization.*) I fell right into that one.

(*Lights dim on* **ARNOLD** *as they rise on the radio...*)

(*Static leads to a loud, unrelenting heavy metal roar...*)

[*"There He Goes" performed by Patsy Cline.**]

(*The music mixes with bar sounds as lights rise on* **ARNOLD** *in the same spot in the bar that Ed occupied earlier.*)

(**ARNOLD** *holds a beer can awkwardly.*)

Look, Murray, I am not that lonely! This here's as far as I go. My limit in a backroom bar is the front room. Maybe I should go home, huh? It's just not my kind of thing, ya know? I realize you may find this hard to comprehend, you bein' the way you are, but Murray, I am not that way inclined. I mean, I'm that way inclined, but I'm not *that* way inclined. Ya know what

---

*A license to produce *Torch Song* does not include a performance license for "There He Goes." The publisher and author suggest that the licensee contact ASCAP or BMI to ascertain the music publisher and contact such music publisher to license or acquire permission for performance of the song. If a license or permission is unattainable for "There He Goes," the licensee may not use the song in *Torch Song* but should create an original composition in a similar style or use a similar song in the public domain. For further information, please see Music Use Note on page 3.

I mean, Murray? I don't see sex as a spectator sport. I like that one sneaked kiss on the elevator on the way to a man's apartment. I like the excuses he makes for the mess the place is in. I like the dainty tour while he's dimming the lights and pouring the drinks. I like never finishing those drinks. Because to me, Murray, a lap in a bed is worth three in a bar. Believe it or not, Murray, no one marries sluts. No they don't, Murray. And it hurts me, Murray, to see this multitude of men so starved for affection that they'd have sex in a dirty backroom instead of a bed the way God intended.

I am not a'scared, Murray.

Murray, I am not a'scared.

All right, I'll show you. We'll go back there together. But I'm telling you now, I ain't doin' nothing. All right? All right. Let's go.

> *(Turns to go and then panics.)*

Quick, hold my hand, Murray, I am a'scared. What if nobody back there wants me? It's one thing to go into a regular bar and not get picked up. That happens all the time to lots of different people for lots of different reasons but, Murray, to go into a place like that and get rejected... Look, I know I got qualities that put me above and beyond the norm. I got...

A quick mind, sharp wit, a glowing personality. But, Murray, what if I don't glow in the dark?

No. I'm all right, Murray. Hey! It's gonna take more than a couple of dozen half-naked men in a pitch-black room to scare me off. Let us go.

> **(ARNOLD** *turns around. The lights dim, leaving him in the glow of a red spotlight.)*

(Feeling around in the dark.) Murray? Where are you? Murray? Murray? Oh, there you are.

Well, it certainly is dark back here.

(Suddenly freezing up.) Murray? Murray? Someone's got his hand on my heinie. Can you see what he looks like?

Yes, Murray, it does make a difference.

Murray. Murray. He's reaching around front and opening my belt.

Murray. Murray. He's opening my zipper.

Murray. Oh, Murray. What am I supposed to do with the beer can?

> *(He bends to put the can on the ground when he is suddenly penetrated.)*

Oh, Murray!

> *(At first **ARNOLD**'s face is twisted in pain and embarrassment as he sways with the humping rhythm of his "partner." He feels out the rhythm and tries to go with it. He tries to smile and look casual about it all. He bounces along, unaffected, almost bored. He looks around and then...)*

(Conversationally.) You come here a lot?

> *(The "partner" hits him on the shoulder.)*

No. I don't have to talk. I mean, it's not part of my fantasy or anything like that. Conversation, that is. Though I must admit being prone to sweet nothings deftly whispered in my ear...

> *(Hit again.)*

But they're not essential to my enjoyment of the love-making experience if you get my drift. You do?

> *(Hit again.)*

But you'd rather I shut up anyway. Fine. I'm not offended. I realize that it must take a lot of concentration for you to keep your concentration in a situation like this so I won't say another word. Okay? Okay.

> *(**ARNOLD** bounces along silently. Looks around and then fumbles for a cigarette. He takes one out...)*

Cigarette?

(Hit again.)

ARNOLD. I'll save you one for later. You mind if I? That's very understanding of you.

> (**ARNOLD** *takes out a match and tries to light his cigarette, but the humping is throwing him off. He reaches around and grabs the "partner's" butt to make him stop. He lights his cigarette and signals the humping to continue.)*

> *(He smokes, looks around...)*

I can't wait to see what you look like.

> *(The "partner" withdraws suddenly.* **ARNOLD** *gasps.)*

Oh! Finished? Already? You must've been hot to trot.

> *(Pulling his clothes back on.)*

Listen, before we go, I'd like you to meet this friend of mine who brought me here tonight. He must be right around here somewhere. Murray? Murray?

Oh, there you are. Murray, I would like you to meet... Y'know, I never did get your name.

> *(The "partner" has split.)*

Hello? Yoo-hoo. And you wonder what's wrong with a place like this? You meet a nice guy and you can't even find him 'cause it's so dark. Oh, duh, he's probably waiting for me out at the bar...

What'd'ya mean, he ain't there? I'm sure he really liked me. He made love to me, didn't he? Murray, he did, didn't he?

> *(Reality seeps in.)*

So, let's go.

> (**ARNOLD** *turns and the brighter bar lights return. He squints, strikes a careless pose, and...)*

Well, at least I don't have to cook him breakfast.

     (Lights fade as the music pumps up from the radio in the dressing room...)

     ["Careless Love" performed by Bessie Smith.]

     (Lights come up on Arnold's dressing table. **ED** *enters the room, looks around uncomfortably. He sits down in the chair by the mirror and fusses with the makeup there.)*

     (ARNOLD *enters, turns the radio off.* **ED** *jumps.)*

Careful. Beauty is addictive.

ED. *(Jumping up.)* You scared me. Hi.

ARNOLD. Hi.

     (ARNOLD *moves past* **ED** *to the dressing table.)*

ED. Bet you thought you'd never see me again. The stage manager said it'd be all right for me to wait for you here. You don't mind, do you? When I asked for you as Arnold he didn't know who I meant. You look beautiful. Really. Lost a little weight...?

     (Reaching out.)

ARNOLD. *(Stiffening.)* Please...

ED. Sorry. I guess you're still angry, huh?

ARNOLD. No, not still angry. This here is brand new. What do you want?

ED. I wanted to see you. I've been worried about you. I wanted to make sure you were all right.

ARNOLD. Five months ago you checked out on me with a single phone call. You said that you knew what you wanted and I wasn't it. Not a word from you since. What do you want?

---

*A license to produce *Torch Song* does not include a performance license for "Careless Love." The publisher and author suggest that the licensee contact ASCAP or BMI to ascertain the music publisher and contact such music publisher to license or acquire permission for performance of the song. If a license or permission is unattainable for "Careless Love," the licensee may not use the song in *Torch Song* but should create an original composition in a similar style or use a similar song in the public domain. For further information, please see Music Use Note on page 3.

ED. To see you.

ARNOLD. Done. Get out.

ED. Arnold, please. I'd like to talk to you.

ARNOLD. No.

ED. Just listen for a minute. It has nothing to do with us.

ARNOLD. The one nice thing I could say about you was when you left, you left.

ED. I told you I wanted us to be friends. You mean a lot to me.

> (**ED** *makes the "I Love You" sign with his hand.*)

ARNOLD. Don't get cute with me.

ED. Maybe I shouldn't have come, but as long as the harm's done can't I talk to you? Just while you dress. It's important to me.

> (**ARNOLD** *points behind him.* **ED** *looks around. There is a stool covered with some clothes. He pulls it up and sits.*)

ED. So... How've you been?

ARNOLD. Could we skip the little niceties and get to the meat.

ED. There is, but... It's not the kind of thing you blurt right out.

ARNOLD. *(Resigned.)* So, how are the folks?

ED. Great. My dad had a little trouble with an ear infection, but it cleared up nicely.

ARNOLD. They go back south for the winter?

ED. Two days ago.

ARNOLD. Two? What took you so long?

ED. What?

ARNOLD. Ed, forget it. It's over. You're not coming back.

ED. I don't want to come back. Really. Things are going fine with Laurel. We spent a really fantastic summer upstate with my folks. We even used their place in Florida for a week.

(*Pause.*)

At first things were a little strained. She'd hang around me all the time wanting us to do everything together. But I talked to her.

(*Pause.*)

Mid-August my sister came up with her two kids and Laurel was great with them. Actually, it was a marvelous experience for both of us. Almost like having a family of our own.

ARNOLD. Sounds wonderful. Pa out in the fields. Ma tendin' to the young'uns. Grandma and Grandpa swingin' on the porch.

ED. It was nice. A good summer. I thought about you a lot up there. You would have liked it.

ARNOLD. Not really the farm girl type.

ED. No. You would have loved it. I worried about you; how you were getting on.

ARNOLD. You could have called and found out.

ED. I wanted to. I thought about it. Once, when everyone was out of the house I even started dialing. I didn't want to build up your hopes.

ARNOLD. Oh, Ed, when I think about you there's only one thing I regret.

ED. What's that?

ARNOLD. That I never beat the shit out of you.

ED. Maybe I'd better go.

ARNOLD. No. Stay. Please. I'm sorry. I was having a little fun. Someone has to. Come back. Sit down.

(**ED** *does as told.*)

So… How's your sex life?

ED. You're doing it again; asking questions you really don't want the answers to.

ARNOLD. Maybe I do.

ED. Arnold, I'm not sure the sex we had was always as good for me as it was for you. Sometimes I think it got out of control. Those last few times, it was like losing myself. I remember once, I don't even think I was fully conscious. All I remember was kissing you and then nothing until waking up in your arms, my body all wet...

ARNOLD. And that's bad?

ED. It's not what I want.

ARNOLD. Funny, it's what I pray for.

ED. That's fine when you're twenty-five. I'm going on thirty-five. I have other needs.

ARNOLD. Where would you be if I was a woman?

ED. What?

ARNOLD. If I was a woman, would you even have looked at her?

ED. I love her, Arnold.

ARNOLD. Like you loved me?

ED. Like I could never love you.

ARNOLD. Good to know.

(*Long silence between them.*)

ED. (*Quietly.*) Sometimes... Sometimes when I have trouble reaching orgasm I imagine you behind me just about to...

ARNOLD. Stop. She doesn't know.

ED. No.

ARNOLD. Does she know anything about me at all?

ED. Your name. She found one of the drawings you made. The one of the tree outside my dining room window. She may know more.

I saw her looking at the music book you gave me. She didn't say anything, but remember you wrote poems to me on half the pages.

(*Pause.*)

I couldn't, Arnold. It's not what I want.

ARNOLD. What was it you wanted to tell me? Huh? Talk to me. I'll understand.

ED. No. It's just a dream I had last week. Nothing really. I dreamt I was in my parents' house and I went down to my father's workshop and got an old rag and a can of turpentine. Then I went to the kitchen and got a plastic bag. I took it all up to my bedroom where I soaked the rag in turpentine and put it into the plastic bag.

Then I made myself comfortable in bed, pulled the covers right up to my neck, and put the plastic bag over my face. The funny part was; while I was gathering the stuff, while I got into bed, while I was blacking out from the fumes...I was happy. Laughing up a storm.

The phone woke me in the morning. It was Laurel. I couldn't understand what she was saying. Half of me was trying to listen to her, half was still in the dream. I put my hand out to steady myself and there, on the pillow, was the plastic bag with the turpentine soaked rag.

I couldn't tell anyone else about it.

(Taking **ARNOLD***'s hand.)*

This is what I've always wanted: You and me together talking. I think I love you more now than ever.

*(***ARNOLD*** jumps to his feet and begins pummeling* **ED***, who reaches out and pulls* **ARNOLD** *into his chest. They embrace desperately.)*

I'm so scared. I need you.

ARNOLD. Okay. Time out. Everyone back to his corner.

*(***ED*** sits back on his stool. ***ARNOLD*** sits on his chair and, as in the opening poses...)*

Wha' happened?

(To **ED***.)* Better?

ED. Yes.

ARNOLD. Good. Then get out! Do you have any idea of what the last five months have been like for me? I cried on so many shoulders... I'm sure I lost half my friends. But I always knew you'd be back. But I thought, when you did, I thought you'd have your shit together. But here you are more fucked up than ever.

(Considering.) Have you got your car with you?

(ED nods.)

I'll get dressed and meet you out front.

ED. You want me to drive you home?

(Strangely happy.) I'll go get the car.

(ED leaves.)

(ARNOLD snaps to and begins cleaning off his face again. He suddenly stops... Turns toward the audience and studies as many faces as he can for answers...)

ARNOLD. So, what now, huh? If I take him back now, knowing all I do, maybe I could make it work. With a little understanding. Maybe a shrink?

I could just let him drive me home and then I could say something like, "The next time you feel like saying I Love You to someone, say it to yourself and see if you believe it." No. That'd go over his head. I think it went over mine.

Or maybe I'll just leave him waiting out there in the cold. I could slip out the back and really cross him out of my life. I'm sure I'd be over him in a few more months, give or take a few more friends.

I don't know.

'Cause if I do start with him again, who's to say he won't keep this shit up? Right? I don't know. Maybe it's what I want. What if he's treating me just the way I want him to?

What if it's me using him to give me that tragic torch singer status I admire so in others? If that's true, then he's my International Stud. Wouldn't that be a kick in the rubber parts? I love him.

So what are you going to do?

But do I love him enough?

What is enough?
(With determination.) This is enough.
(Making the sign with his hands.) Enough.

    (Light shift.)

["Fugue in G Minor" by J. S. Bach begins to play through the Bakelite radio. It is performed by a brass quartet.*]

(A huge bed appears upstage.)

*(**ED**, propped up with pillows and reading a newspaper, sits regally atop the bed. He lifts the covers next to him, inviting **ARNOLD** in.)*

(The light box that reads "The International Stud" flickers and shorts out.)

*(**ARNOLD** walks upstage to meet the bed, climbs on top, and takes his place beside **ED**.)*

(The light box flickers back to life:)

"FUGUE IN A NURSERY" Summer 1975

*(**ARNOLD** slips down under the covers.)*

*(**LAUREL** sits up from under the covers on the other side of **ED**.)*

(The music resolves...)

[Note: Bits of Bach's "Fugue" can be used throughout as punctuation or to aid in separating scenes from one another.]

LAUREL. Isn't this civilized? Do you think they have enough blankets? Maybe I should...

ED. They'll be fine.

LAUREL. But it gets awfully cold in there...

ED. Laurel, they'll be fine.

---

*A license to produce *Torch Song* does not include a performance license for any copyrighted versions of "Fugue in G Minor" performed by a brass quartet. The publisher and author suggest that the licensee contact ASCAP or BMI to ascertain the music publisher and contact such music publisher to license or acquire permission for performance of the song. If a license or permission is unattainable for any copyrighted versions of "Fugue in G Minor" performed by a brass quartet, the licensee may not use the song in *Torch Song* but should create an original composition in a similar style or use a similar song in the public domain. For further information, please see Music Use Note on page 3.

LAUREL. All right. Don't be so grouchy.

> *(Cuddling.)*

Wanna...?

ED. Didn't you say you had some paperwork to finish?

LAUREL. I'm too excited.

> *(Snatching his paper.)*

Don't you wanna...?

ED. Can I have my paper?

LAUREL. You're an old fart, you know that?

> *(Returning the paper.)*

This is just so civilized. Guests up to our country home for the weekend. I can't tell you how excited I am.

ED. We've had guests before.

LAUREL. I'd hardly compare this to having your sister and the kids up. Imagine being hostess to your lover's ex and his new boyfriend. It's downright Noël Coward. How's your English accent? I think we should use English accents all weekend.

ED. Would you stop?

LAUREL. I'm excited. That's all.

ED. This is not the weekend I had planned.

LAUREL. I have no idea what you're talking about.

ED. Alan. That's what I'm talking about. I should have known Arnold would pull something like this.

LAUREL. Arnold asked if he could bring a friend and I told him he could...

ED. You had no right to. This weekend was supposed to be just the three of us.

LAUREL. What's the big deal. We've got enough food for four. I didn't have to open another room or anything. What was Arnold supposed to do – Watch us toddle off to bed while he slept alone?

ED. Did you catch the way he fawned over him at dinner? He practically cut his steak for him.

LAUREL. No more than I fawned over you. And I did cut your steak.

ED. I could have killed you for that.

LAUREL. You're being ridiculous. There are bound to be compensations on all four of our parts. Little games and jealousies are going to pop up. But I'm positive it's going to be a great weekend.

ED. Did you see how he made such a point of running off to bed early? "I'm so tired. All that good food has done me in." His hands all over the boy.

LAUREL. Well, if I had something as pretty as that to go to bed with, I wouldn't stay up late either.

ED. You really think he's pretty? You don't think he's a little young?

LAUREL. You hear the way their bed springs were squeaking?

ED. I think I do pretty well in the squeaking department given allowances for wear and tear...

LAUREL. It's a little early in the race to be making excuses, don't you think?

ED. You want to race? All right, let's race. And may the best man win!

LAUREL. And now, Ladies and Gentlemen, driving a 1968 Serta orthopedic...

ED. On your marks... Set... Go!

> (**ED** *pulls the covers over them, which exposes* **ALAN** *on the other side of the bed. He bolts upright, a look of panic on his face.*)
>
> (*He takes a moment to place himself and then begins to search for* **ARNOLD** *under the covers. He pulls the blankets off* **ARNOLD** *and speaks right into his face...*)

ALAN. Are you asleep?

ARNOLD. God, you're gorgeous. Now go away.

ALAN. Come on. Wake up.

ARNOLD. But I'm having this flawless dream.

ALAN. About me?

ARNOLD. If it is, can I go back to sleep?

ALAN. Yes.

ARNOLD. All about you.

ALAN. What about me?

ARNOLD. *(Suddenly feeling the boy's presence.)* You really are awake.

ALAN. That doesn't matter.

ARNOLD. Maybe not to you.

ALAN. Tell me the dream.

ARNOLD. If you like it, can we...?

ALAN. No.

ARNOLD. Then I'm going back to sleep.

ALAN. Then I'm going to see if anyone else is up.

ARNOLD. Give my best to the bisexuals.

ALAN. Only he's bisexual. She's straight.

ARNOLD. Too bad. Mixed marriages never work.

ALAN. Then what were you doing with him?

ARNOLD. Slumming.

ALAN. And what are you doing with me?

ARNOLD. Nothing. It's gone!

ALAN. It'll be back.

ARNOLD. But it won't be the same.

ALAN. Of course it will.

ARNOLD. Do you ever think before you speak?

ALAN. No. Do you?

ARNOLD. Frequently. It helps pass the time while you're speaking.

ALAN. Tell me the dream.

ARNOLD. How old are you?

ALAN. You know how old I am.

ARNOLD. Tell me again. I need reassurance. Why's it still dark out?

ALAN. It's nighttime. Do you mind?

ARNOLD. Of course not.

> *(Taking **ALAN** into his arms.)*

What frightened you?

ALAN. Nothing. I just felt like talking. Did Ed ever have bad dreams?

ARNOLD. Everyone does.

ALAN. Get me a dog.

ARNOLD. Why?

ALAN. I want one.

ARNOLD. I don't give you things.

ALAN. Yes, you do. No, you don't. But a dog's not a thing.

ARNOLD. I have no money for a dog.

ALAN. Sometimes they have dogs for adoption in the paper. Where's that newspaper?

ARNOLD. Under the bed. Is that what you tell the other models at the studio; that I buy you things?

ALAN. No.

ARNOLD. Don't do that to yourself; treat yourself like a piece of meat. That's what all those leering faggots do, so you don't have to do it to yourself.

ALAN. I don't.

ARNOLD. You're so much more than that. You're smart and ambitious. You don't have to be a model.

ALAN. You don't have to be a drag queen.

ARNOLD. Not the same thing at all. A model IS. A drag queen ASPIRES.

ALAN. Would you stop? Where's the paper?

ARNOLD. *(Slapping it into his hands.)* Here.

ALAN. I love you.

> *(The covers fly off the other side of the bed,*
> *exposing **ED** and **LAUREL** post-coitus.)*

LAUREL. I don't believe I've seen you this turned on in months. If that's Arnold's effect on you then I'm asking him to move in.

ED. It's not Arnold, it's you.

LAUREL. Is that why you called me Arnold?

ED. I did not.

LAUREL. You certainly did. Deep into loving you whispered in my ear, "I love you, Arnold."

ED. That's not funny. You shouldn't make up things like that.

LAUREL. Fine. I misheard you. Take it easy.

ED. It's that damned kid. This was going to be a perfect weekend; just the three of us. I thought, seeing you two together... I thought I'd be able to put a period on that whole chapter of my life. But the second he walked through the door I knew the period had been there long ago and this whole weekend was for nothing.

LAUREL. I'm glad you've made up your mind.

ED. I didn't mean... I wasn't planning on comparing the two of you. Leave it to Arnold to bring that kid.

LAUREL. He also brought a cake, a lace tablecloth and a copy of the *Village Voice*. Enjoy them all.

ED. Come here and I'll read you the funny pages.

LAUREL. I have my own reading, thank you.

(*Back on the other side of the bed,* **ALAN** *and* **ARNOLD** *are still cuddling...*)

ARNOLD. This was my room. I mean, we slept together in there, but I kept my stuff in here in case any neighbors or family snooped around.

ALAN. Did you really love him?

ARNOLD. I guess.

ALAN. And he loved you.

ARNOLD. I wouldn't say that.

ALAN. I would. I see the way he looks at you. Why'd you two break up?

ARNOLD. We wanted different things.

ALAN. Like what?

ARNOLD. I wanted a husband and he wanted a wife.

ALAN. You ever think of going back?

ARNOLD. You can't go back.

ALAN. Why not?

ARNOLD. Because.

ALAN. Because why?

ARNOLD. Good thing I was not your mother. I could have denied you nothing. I am in awe that she denied you as much as she did for you to need to ask for so much now.

ALAN. Ssshhh! I thought I heard someone talking.

ARNOLD. Probably Ed talking in his sleep.

ALAN. He talks in his sleep?

ARNOLD. Talks, screams, kicks, plays with puppets...

ALAN. You really loved him, huh?

ARNOLD. Again?

ALAN. I'm curious. Why?

ARNOLD. Why? Why does anyone love anyone? Because I did. Because...I did. Because...he let me. Now, talk dirty to me.

　　　　　(**LAUREL** *and* **ALAN** *appear isolated in the light.*)

LAUREL. So, tell me about yourself.

ALAN. I'm a model. Clothes, toothpaste... Whatever they can sell with an All-American puss.

LAUREL. And where'd you grow up?

ALAN. Arnold says I haven't.

LAUREL. You two must be very happy together.

ALAN. There are easier things than living with Arnold. He thinks it's immoral, that it makes him a lesser person to be with me because I'm good-looking.

LAUREL. Come on...

ALAN. Really. He'd be much happier if I was his age, his size, his...size. Sometimes I'm not sure if he wants a boyfriend or a bookend.

LAUREL. It's good that you have a sense of humor. Ed has none. But that's part of his charm.

ALAN. No wonder they didn't last.

LAUREL. There's possibly more to it than that. Did you know that they were still seeing each other when I met Ed? I didn't. Friends introduced us. I had just come through a rather bad relationship with a man who turned out to be bisexual. The bi leaning more toward the new boyfriend. I was quite a mess. He wasn't the first unavailable man I'd dated. My therapist thought I should take a break and just work on me. But then my friend Janet said she knew this handsomely available teacher named Ed, so...I said yes. She set it up. And here we are.

ALAN. A real live blind date.

LAUREL. Blind. Right. We'd been going out for more than a month before he told me about Arnold. By then it was too late to give up without a fight.

ALAN. A fight?

LAUREL. Not a fight. There was no fight. I just pulled back enough to let Ed feel his freedom. No commitments. No pressure. Soon he was telling me that he wanted to end his relationship with Arnold so I suggested he speak to my therapist and that was that.

*(**ED** and **ARNOLD** are now together.)*

ARNOLD. You never told me about a shrink.

ED. I know how you feel about them. But she's been very supportive. Never pushed me toward any decision I didn't want to make.

ARNOLD. So, you're straight now?

ED. Not now. I always have been.

ARNOLD. And me, and all the others...? What were we; a phase you were going through?

ED. For you, everyone is either gay or in the closet.

ARNOLD. I could've kept you.

ED. You think so? In all of my time with Laurel I've never cheated on her once. And believe me, our relationship allows for it.

ARNOLD. If your relationship allows for it then it isn't cheating.

ED. Are you making a pass at me?

(They both laugh.)

You don't love that kid.

ARNOLD. Says you. What makes you think I'm in love with anyone?

ED. Because we've been lying in bed together for over an hour in and out of each other's arms and you've yet to make a pass at me.

ARNOLD. That's not love. That's good taste! You and Laurel working on having kids yet?

ED. No.

ARNOLD. Don't you still want kids?

ED. Laurel thinks we should wait. Why rush?

ARNOLD. Do you remember that woman we met at that party? She arranged for gay couples to take foster kids? You probably don't remember, you said you wanted a boy, but you were gay then.

ED. That was just talk. A fantasy.

ARNOLD. Is that what it was?

ED. Sure. Like having our own island, or airplane...

ARNOLD. Or relationship.

ED. That was one of the best things about being with you. I could fantasize about anything. Let my mind go off as far as it could, and there you were all caught up with me, making it almost real.

ARNOLD. 'Cause I didn't know it wasn't. They weren't fantasies to me. Possibilities. None of it impossible. I have a ledger where I write things like that down. And when I get something on the list I put a check-mark next to it. I must have a dozen pages filled with my possibilities. And you'd be surprised how many check-marks there are too. Oh, they're little things like an electric toothbrush or an azalea bush or a subscription to *National Geographic* but they each mark an achievement for me.

ED. Am I on that list?

ARNOLD. Listed and checked off.

ED. That's cheating. You don't have me.

ARNOLD. Don't I?

ED. No.

ARNOLD. I'll be sure to correct my ledger first thing Monday morning.

(*All four are in focus now.*)

LAUREL. Ed? Would you like to help me clear the table?

ARNOLD. I can do that.

LAUREL. Don't be silly. You're a guest. Ed, why don't you take Arnold and Alan out to the barn and show them our new canning machine? We've been canning all our own vegetables for two years.

ARNOLD. Ed never said a word. But you know how modest he is. Ed, why don't you take Alan out and show it to him. He's the real can connoisseur in the family. I'll stay behind and visit. We've yet to have a moment alone to compare notes on you.

ED. Just what she's been waiting for.

LAUREL. Ed!

ED. (*To* **ALAN.**) Why don't you grab that bottle of brandy. No need for us to rough it.

(*A sudden shift in lights catches* **ALAN** *and* **ARNOLD** *alone, mid-fight.*)

ALAN. Start packing. We're getting out of here tonight.

ARNOLD. Would you stop?

ALAN. What was I supposed to do? You deserted me all afternoon.

ARNOLD. Less than an hour. And I didn't desert you. We were in the kitchen doing dishes. If you were lonely you should have come in.

ALAN. Oh, I wasn't lonely.

     (**ARNOLD** *turns away to face* **LAUREL.** **ALAN** *fades into the darkness.*)

ARNOLD. Isn't this civilized? Doing the dishes.

     (*Looking at his reflection in a plate.*)

Platter, platter on the stack. Does she think I want him back?

LAUREL. You work fast. I thought we'd kind of waltz around the table a few times first. So, do you?

ARNOLD. What do you think?

LAUREL. I think you do.

ARNOLD. Really? Why?

LAUREL. You're here, aren't you?

ARNOLD. You asked me to come.

LAUREL. You didn't have to. Look, I know you don't love Alan.

ARNOLD. I keep hearing that.

LAUREL. How could you when you're still in love with Ed? I know that from the start you cared for Ed more than he did for you.

ARNOLD. He told you that?

LAUREL. It's nothing to be ashamed of.

ARNOLD. Of course not. If it's true that one person always loves more than the other, why not be the one who feels the most? But that doesn't mean I still feel that way.

LAUREL. Then why do you call him all the time? I know about your calls in the afternoon when I'm at work.

ARNOLD. He told you I call him?

LAUREL. It's the kind of relationship we have.

ARNOLD. Laurel, I don't want you to misunderstand and think I'm calling Ed a liar but...I've never called him. Yes, we've spoken, but it's always been him calling me. He'd call and tell me how happy you two were, all about his family (none of whom I've ever met), and I'd say a nice little goodbye and that was that.

LAUREL. Then why'd you come up here?

ARNOLD. To see how my paint job was holding up. Y'know I painted this room. Took me days. I was so scared I'd drip on the "original wide plank oak" floors.

LAUREL. I'm sorry. I'm obviously pushing you to admit something you're not ready to face.

ARNOLD. You're pushing all right, but I don't think you know toward what. Laurel, are you happy with Ed?

LAUREL. The happiest I've ever been in my life.

ARNOLD. Then, what more do you want?

> *(Lights out on them and up on* **ALAN** *and* **ED** *as they pass the brandy bottle back and forth.)*

ALAN. To own a disco. I knew this guy, he was a few years older than me, who'd met this older guy who set him up in business. I figured I could do the same. But when I made my entrance into the Big Apple, and believe me, fourteen-year-old gay boys make quite an entrance into any apple, I found that no one was interested in my business plan. No one was interested in anything much beyond my price tag for the evening. See, people with a taste for fourteen-year-olds are used to paying for it and consider a freebie suspicious if not downright immoral so I became a hustler. I figured I needed the affection more than they needed the money. Now, of course, things are different, but then...? Anyway, the hustling led to some connections, the connections to the modeling, the modeling to...

ED. Arnold.

ALAN. No, Arnold was more of a detour. One night I was out drinking with a friend and got more than usually polluted. Somehow I ended up in a Lower East Side bar that had a drag show.

Anyway, I got into a fight with this big guy who threw me down across a table, jumped up onto my chest and put a knife to my neck. Everyone was screaming and crowding around to watch me get cut when, all of a sudden, there was silence. The crowd parted to make an aisle and, up through it like Moses parting the Red Sea, came this Amazon woman.

I'd never seen anything like her. She was beautiful. Not like pretty beautiful, but like mountain beautiful. She put her hand out to the guy, he handed over the knife and was gone. No words. No nothing.

ED. Did you realize right away that it was a guy?

ALAN. I was too drunk that night to realize I was a guy. I fell on that discovery the next morning. And we've been together ever since. Now tell me about you. That's why we're here.

ED. Is it?

ALAN. Arnold didn't want to come, but I wasn't going to let this opportunity to see my competition go by.

ED. I'm no competition.

ALAN. That's what I was thinking. So, tell me about you?

ED. I'm sure Arnold had plenty to say on the subject.

ALAN. He said you're a self-centered, insensitive, boring fool who wouldn't know love if it wore wings, a diaper, and shot heart-shaped arrows at your butt.

ED. Meaning himself?

ALAN. Meaning himself. Anything you'd care to add.

ED. No. That'll do. And what do you think?

ALAN. I think I'll reserve judgment until I can make a closer inspection.

(**ED** *lies down next to* **ALAN**.)

ED. Close enough?

ALAN. Too close for comfort. You asked me to sit in the hay, not roll in it.

ED. It was a two-part question. I think you're very beautiful.

ALAN. I thought you were reformed.

ED. I'm not proposing marriage.

(*Gently pulling* **ALAN** *closer*.)

If you want me to stop just say so. Do you?

(No resistance.)

I didn't think so.

(ALAN and ED sink back onto the bed as ARNOLD pops up excitedly...)

ARNOLD. I don't know when to stop. That's my problem. I didn't come up here to hurt her. I didn't even come up here to hurt him, (though that would have been all right). I was so proud of myself up 'til now. I thought I was handling myself so maturely. I guess I was saving it all up for that.

(To the invisible ALAN.) I hope you're enjoying yourself.

ALAN. *(From under the covers.)* I am.

ARNOLD. Good, 'cause it's all your fault. Why couldn't I just keep my trap shut? I've always thought of myself as a kind person. Not saintly, but generously thoughtful in a bitchy sort of way. Well, she asked for it. She begged for it. And, boy, did I give it to her. Point after pointless point I pointed out that, without a doubt, Ed has no idea that she actually exists. That to him she is simply proof of his normality. And she took it. Stood there staring me straight in the eye and listened to every word...

(Realizing he's still alone.)

Well, get over here and comfort me! Can't you see I am disturbed?

(ALAN crawls over and puts his arms around ARNOLD.)

ALAN. Why should I if you're such a rat?

ARNOLD. Because the innocent must suffer, not the guilty. This is America. God, you smell good.

ALAN. Better than him?

ARNOLD. You know he's jealous of you. Told me so himself.

ALAN. You shouldn't have left me alone all afternoon. How do you think I felt?

ARNOLD. How'd you feel?

ALAN. I came up here to be with you, not him. Let's get out of here.

> (**ALAN** *dives under the covers.* **ARNOLD** *is alone for a puzzling moment and then goes under the covers as well.*)
>
> (*Lights shift.*)
>
> (**LAUREL** *sits, center of the bed, staring out into space.*)
>
> (*Telephone rings.*)
>
> (**ARNOLD** *reaches around under the covers until he finds the receiver...*)

ARNOLD. Happy home for the bewildered.

ED. Hi. I woke you.

ARNOLD. Oh, hi. Listen, I was going to call you later and thank you for the weekend...

ED. I just wanted to make sure you got home all right.

ARNOLD. Fine. Drove straight through.

ED. I really enjoyed having you up here. So did Laurel. We learned a lot about our relationship.

ARNOLD. Holding seminars?

ED. Could you be nice?

ARNOLD. Sorry. Morning breath.

ED. Is Alan there with you?

ARNOLD. No. He dropped me off then drove out to Queens to bring the car back to his mother. Must have spent the night.

ED. But he's coming back.

ARNOLD. I guess. What's the difference?

ED. Curious. That's all.

ARNOLD. Is something wrong? You sound funny which, for you, is a stretch.

ED. I have a favor. Laurel went into the city for a few days. She needed to check on some classes. Anyway, I thought it might be nice if you had her over for dinner or met her for lunch or something.

ARNOLD. Shit. Look, Ed, I'm really sorry I caused...

ED. No. We didn't have words or anything. We both thought we could use a little time alone to think about our relationship. I love her very much.

ARNOLD. Have you tried telling her that?

ED. She's not like you, Arnold. She doesn't need to be reassured every hour on the hour.

(**ARNOLD** *bites his tongue.*)

Will you see her? I'd appreciate it. And one more thing...

ARNOLD. Well, speak up. I'm a drag queen not a mind reader.

ED. Remember that thing we talked about? That list? I told you to erase the check-mark next to my name.

ARNOLD. Ed, I just got home. I told you I'd...

ED. Don't. I mean, if you want you can leave the check-mark.

(**ED**'s *light fades out and* **ARNOLD** *is alone with* **LAUREL**.)

LAUREL. So, what'd you say?

ARNOLD. I told him I'd leave the check-mark but erase the name.

LAUREL. You didn't.

ARNOLD. I didn't. But I should have. Sometimes I get the feeling he's learning. Are you going back to him?

LAUREL. How about you and Alan? You're wonderful together. I'm sure everything will work itself out.

ARNOLD. I didn't know there was anything that needed working out.

LAUREL. What happened between Alan and Ed doesn't bother you at all?

(*Suddenly* **ED** *and* **ALAN** *are in the picture as well...*)

ED. You blurted it out just like that?

LAUREL. I thought he knew.

ALAN. I tried to tell you.

ARNOLD. Who listens to you?

LAUREL. Why did you think I left?

ARNOLD. I thought it was something I said.

ALAN. *(To* **ED.***)* Are you going to tell Laurel.

ED. What I do is my own business.

ARNOLD. *(To* **LAUREL.***)* You saw them together?

LAUREL. Ed told me after you left. I was stripping the beds. He sat me down and said he had something to discuss. He said he was sorry. Not that he'd done it, but that he had to tell me about it. I was dumbstruck. He was crying. I didn't know which of us to comfort, so I sat there. After a while he left the room, I packed my bag and left. It seemed like the right thing to do. There I was packed, at the door, so I left. So, this is the nursery. It's not at all what I'd expected from Ed's description. I like it though. It's got a coziness...a warmth. I can feel it.

ARNOLD. Thanks.

LAUREL. If this is the nursery, does that make you the nurse?

ARNOLD. Registered with the A.M.A. Hurts, huh?

LAUREL. Like a claw in my stomach. Just once in my life I'd like to have an affair go on the rocks after the passion wears off; when I'm bored with the routine, the sex, the talk. I'd love to know what it feels like to have the flame rekindled by jealousy instead of this...having the rug pulled out from under me like this. Just once I'd like to be standing on sure ground when the blow hits instead of crawling around on my hands and knees like a baby.

ALAN. All you had to do was ask me.

ARNOLD. Ask you what?

ALAN. Not to fool around and I wouldn't have.

ED. Because I wanted you to feel that you could.

LAUREL. Obviously you wanted me to feel that you could.

ALAN. It's the kind of relationship you said you want.

ARNOLD. Just because I said it's what I want doesn't mean that's what I want. I mean, it's what I want but it doesn't mean I'm ready for it.

ED. You're being ridiculous.

ARNOLD. Well, there you have it.

ALAN. There I have what?

ARNOLD. *(To* **LAUREL**.*)* It's my fault. I'm lousy in bed. It's true. I never relax enough. I guess I'm just an old-fashioned kind of guy; I hardly ever enjoy sex with someone I know.

> *(**LAUREL** and **ED** move closer to one another as **ALAN** comes to **ARNOLD**.)*

ALAN. She'll stay. They were made for each other.

LAUREL. I owe him a chance.

ARNOLD. It's wrong.

LAUREL. What do I have to lose?

ARNOLD. It's all wrong.

LAUREL. Otherwise what was it for?

ARNOLD. I can't tell you how strongly I feel that it's wrong. You were wrong to do what you did. Though I know why you did. And Ed was wrong to do what he did. Though I know why he did. And Laurel was wrong to use what you two did. Though I know why she did. And I was wrong to do everything I did. But I did. I don't know. If two wrongs don't make a right, maybe four do.

ALAN. Who cares? I've got what I want.

ARNOLD. You're awful pushy for a kid not old enough to pee straight. Come on, talk dirty to me.

ALAN. Wait. One more thing I want to ask you.

ARNOLD. The answer is yes.

ALAN. You don't know the question.

ARNOLD. Doesn't matter. I'm too tired to argue about anything. So whatever the question, my answer is yes.

ALAN. Good. I love you, too.

ARNOLD. Oh, Alan. Why do you have to…

ALAN. Shut up! Can't you take a joke?

> *("Fugue" concludes as the lights go to black.)*
> *(The light box sputters and then announces:)*
> **"INTERMISSION"**

ACT TWO

Scene One

(The preset lighting features a spotlight on the Bakelite radio.)

["Cooking Breakfast for the One I Love" performed by Fanny Brice.]*

(The light box flickers and sputters and finally announces:)

"WIDOWS AND CHILDREN FIRST" June 1980

(Lights rise on an almost conventional sitcom set of a living room/kitchen. There's a front door, a door to the bathroom, and a doorway leading to the bedrooms. The details that make this apartment unique are the number of rabbit objects around the room. There are rabbit pillows, figurines, mugs, throw rugs... Even the walls have rabbit-themed stencilling.)

*(As the curtain rises, **ED** is cooking at the stove.)*

---

*A license to produce *Torch Song* does not include a performance license for "Cooking Breakfast for the One I Love." The publisher and author suggest that the licensee contact ASCAP or BMI to ascertain the music publisher and contact such music publisher to license or acquire permission for performance of the song. If a license or permission is unattainable for "Cooking Breakfast for the One I Love," the licensee may not use the song in *Torch Song* but should create an original composition in a similar style or use a similar song in the public domain. For further information, please see Music Use Note on page 3.

RADIO. It's seven-eighteen in the Big Apple and this is Hi Tide wishing you a good morning.

> (*A radio chorus sings:*)

"GOOD MORNING, GOOD MORNING"
And now for all you sleepyheads just shaking off the nighttime blues, number one on our Hot-Pick chart and guaranteed to raise the dead, Edward O. Wilson's "I Was Born This Way, What's Your Excuse?"

ED. (*Snapping off the radio.*) There's a thought to start the day.

DAVID. (*Offstage.*) Arnold? You got anything I can put on my eye?

ED. He's in the bedroom.

DAVID. (*Offstage.*) What?

ED. Arnold's still in the bedroom.

DAVID. (*Offstage.*) Never mind. I found something.

ED. Arnold? You up? Breakfast is on the table.

DAVID. (*Offstage.*) What?

ED. I was talking to Arnold.

> (*A sudden explosion from the stove as the lid pops off a pot.* **ARNOLD**, *in bathrobe and bunny slippers, rushes in...*)

ARNOLD. What the hell...?

ED. Coffee's ready.

ARNOLD. Oh, you're making breakfast. Aren't you an angel. Smells terrible.

ED. My specialty: Eggs, onions and kippered herring en casserole.

ARNOLD. Shame I'm on a diet.

ED. Since when?

ARNOLD. Since I heard your specialty. And David is...?

ED. In the throne room.

ARNOLD. Hurry up, Sugar-Puss, you'll be late for school.

> (*Looking around the kitchen.*)

Since when do you make coffee in a pressure cooker?

ED. Water boils faster.

DAVID. *(Cracking the door open.)* Everybody ready? Stand back and hang onto your apron strings 'cause here I come.

(He enters, modeling a three-piece suit.)

Well? What'cha think?

ARNOLD. What's the occasion? Ms. Schnable isn't due 'til next week.

DAVID. But your mother's due today. And look, I put some gook on. You can't even see the black eye.

ARNOLD. When I think of that kid hitting you…

DAVID. I can take care of myself.

ARNOLD. I see.

ED. How'd you get into a fight?

DAVID. He said something I didn't like so I slugged him.

ED. So how did you end up with the black eye?

DAVID. I never said I slugged him first.

ARNOLD. Meet my son the champ.

DAVID. That's me; Champ David.

ARNOLD. Just stay away from that kid today. I got no money for another suit.

(ARNOLD exits to the bathroom as DAVID sits down for breakfast. ED brings him a plateful.)

DAVID. What died in here?

ED. I cooked it myself. Is there a problem?

DAVID. From me? You kidding? You know me, always ready for a gastronomic adventure. Looks wonderful. Could you pass the salt? How'd you sleep?

ED. That couch and I are not speaking.

DAVID. It's your fourth night. You'll get used to it. Could you pass the pepper? I slept on it for weeks until my room was ready. The secret is to embrace the lumps.

ED. I should be able to find a place by the weekend.

DAVID. Hey, no rush. Can I have the ketchup? It's great having you here. Could you pass the mustard?

ED. Something wrong with the food?

DAVID. Not at all. Very tasty. Could you pass the mayo? *(Off* **ED***'s glare.)* Hold the mayo. Oh, I forgot, your wife called.

ED. When?

DAVID. Middle of the night. I tried to wake you but... Anyway, I told her you'd call back in the morning.

ED. What time was that?

DAVID. Must've been around two. You sure are a heavy sleeper. The phone rang like five times.

ED. I'd better call her. Help yourself to seconds. There's plenty.

DAVID. And I was worried.

ED. What were you doing up so late?

DAVID. Answering the phone.

(**ED** *talks on the phone as* **ARNOLD** *re-enters.*)

ED. Laurel? What's up? ...And that couldn't have waited until morning?

ARNOLD. Hey, Champ, remember to bring your report card back. It's by the door. I signed it.

DAVID. What day is Ms. Schnable coming?

ARNOLD. Every third Thursday for three more months and then you're all mine.

DAVID. And the checks stop.

ARNOLD. I didn't take you in for the money.

DAVID. You're the first.

ARNOLD. Who's on the phone?

DAVID. Ed.

ARNOLD. I thought I recognized the voice.

ED. Laurel, I wish you wouldn't... Not on the phone.

ARNOLD. Don't you hate a one-sided conversation?

DAVID. There's another kind?

ED. Oh, for God's sake. Are you crying?

ARNOLD. Animal.

ED. Fine. I'll come over... I'll call first... Fine. See you then.

DAVID. She gave you a hard time, huh?

> *(Pinched by* **ARNOLD.***)*

Ow. Child abuse!

ARNOLD. Ed, do you think Laurel will let you stay at your place Wednesday? We've got our inspection from Child Welfare and I've got enough to explain without you on the couch.

ED. I'm good enough for your mother but not David's social worker?

ARNOLD. Did I ever say you were good enough for anyone?

DAVID. You look good enough for me.

ARNOLD. David!

ED. You don't want her to meet me because you don't want to have to explain our relationship.

ARNOLD. We have no relationship.

ED. *(Teasing him.)* You don't have to hide me. I promise not to tell her I'm a married man.

ARNOLD. As if.

ED. I think I make a convincing homosexual.

DAVID. You can make this convincing homosexual.

ARNOLD. David! And if she thought you were gay she'd never believe you slept on the couch.

ED. I could show her the scars.

ARNOLD. I could show you the door.

DAVID. I could show you a good time.

ARNOLD & ED. David!

DAVID. Well, I'd love to sit around and chit-chat with you grown-up types but we straight-C students pride ourselves on our punctuality.

ARNOLD. Brush your teeth.

DAVID. Ma!

ARNOLD. Don't Ma me. March. And don't call me Ma in front of my mother.

(**DAVID** *exits to the bathroom as* **ED** *laughs.*)

ARNOLD. Having a good time, Hazel?

ED. You do act like his mother.

ARNOLD. Not at all. I act like *my* mother and I can't make it stop. Honestly, how can one person be mother-father-friend-confessor all rolled into one?

ED. You're doing great. Best mother-father-friend-confessor I've ever seen.

ARNOLD. *(Tasting the food.)* Y'know, this stuff smells awful but it tastes much worse.

(**ARNOLD** *starts washing up the kitchen.*)

ED. You ever wonder what things would be like if I'd never met Laurel? You think we might have stayed together, maybe even have had David?

ARNOLD. Did I meet Alan?

ED. If I didn't meet Laurel you wouldn't have met Alan.

ARNOLD. Oh, so you're in charge?

ED. No. Yeah. Well, that's not what I'm asking. I mean, didn't you ever wonder?

ARNOLD. I guess. When Alan died I thought about a lot of things.

ED. And?

ARNOLD. Ed, I've got enough trouble with the "what nows" without starting in on the "what ifs."

ED. I think we might have been very happy together.

ARNOLD. Or it could have been me that you just walked out on again.

ED. I didn't just walk out on Laurel. And I didn't just walk out on you. People do make mistakes.

ARNOLD. I gotta write that down.

ED. And sometimes they are even forgiven for them.

ARNOLD. I'll forgive you if you put away the bedding on the couch.

ED. Maybe I should find a hotel. You and your mother need some time alone.

ARNOLD. You wouldn't leave me unprotected at a time like this, would you? Of course you would. But you ain't gonna. My mother isn't going to feature the idea of me becoming a father and your professional opinion as a tenured educator will prove invaluable.

ED. She'll say I'm prejudiced.

ARNOLD. She'll say a lot of things. You'll learn not to listen. My mother's all right basically. We've always enjoyed a healthy mother/son relationship. I told her I was gay when I was thirteen.

ED. You knew when you were thirteen?

ARNOLD. When I was thirteen I knew everything.
(Calling out.) David, hurry. You'll be late.

DAVID. *(Offstage.)* Don't rush an artist.

ARNOLD. What was I saying?

ED. Something about your mother.

ARNOLD. My mother: The Sylvia Sidney of Brighton Beach. We always talked, well, until my father died. Then, I don't know, something happened. She clammed up. She refused to talk about it or how she was coping. But Alan had just moved in, so giving me advice kept her busy. Anyway, she retired, moved to Florida...
And then when Alan died I was expected to observe the same vow of silence she'd taken about my father. So our long-distance calls became longer distance calls. I never even told her how Alan was killed. She assumed it was a car accident and I didn't bother correcting her.

ED. And now you don't know how to tell her about David.

ARNOLD. I told her about David. But she assumed he was my roommate...

ED. And you didn't bother correcting her. How bad could it possibly be?

ARNOLD. Stick around, kid.

DAVID. *(Re-entering, showing off his teeth.)* Will these impress Granny?

(Telephone rings.)

ARNOLD. Granny? Granny, David?

DAVID. *(Answering the phone.)* Sister Arnold's House of Hope. You pay, we pray. Brother David speaking.

ARNOLD. *(Grabbing the receiver away.)* Give me that. Hello? ...Oh, hi, Murray.

DAVID. My work here is done. Later, lovebirds.

ARNOLD. *(To DAVID.)* Have you got a comb? A handkerchief?

(DAVID produces both.)

And don't forget your report card.

(DAVID waves the report card but then sees...)

DAVID. What the hell is this?

ARNOLD. Hang on, Murray.

DAVID. *(Reading from the card.)* "I'm proud of his improvement and am sure he'll do even better next year."

ARNOLD. It asked for a parent's comment. I had to write something.

DAVID. No, you didn't!

(DAVID storms off to the bedroom.)

ARNOLD. Murray, can I call you back when I get my little men off to work? ...David, hang up that extension... No, you can't have a divorce. Hang up.

(ARNOLD hangs up the phone and stares at ED.)

All right, what did I do wrong now?

ED. Kids like to brag that they forged their parents' signatures. If there's a sensible comment like that, then everyone will know it's the real thing.

ARNOLD. If you're trying to make me feel old...

DAVID. *(Storming from the bedroom to the front door.)* I'm getting out of here before you think of something else.

ARNOLD. Where are your schoolbooks?

DAVID. In school.

ARNOLD. Hey! Aren't you forgetting something?

DAVID. What now?

ARNOLD. I don't get no kiss goodbye?

> (**DAVID** *laughs and comes back to give* **ARNOLD** *a warm hug and kiss.*)

DAVID. Goodbye. Love you.

ARNOLD. Me too.

DAVID. Have a nice day, Ed. You too...Ma!

> *(And he's gone.)*

ED. Men kissing.

ARNOLD. Aren't you going to work?

ED. Brooklyn Day. My school's closed.

ARNOLD. Perfect. You can stay here and protect me from my mother.

ED. I'm going to run out for the paper. Maybe I can get a lead on an apartment.

ARNOLD. Just to the corner and right back.

ED. Stop. Your mother is going to see you and David and be happy for the both of you.

ARNOLD. I'm doing good with him, right?

ED. You've taken a punk kid who's spent the last three years on the streets and in juvenile court and turned him into a home-living, school-going, fun-loving kid in six months. Yes. I think you're doing great with him.

ARNOLD. Who asked you? Go. And come back!

ED. *(Out the door.)* I won't be long.

> (**ED**'s gone. **ARNOLD** suddenly panics...)

ARNOLD. Ed! Ed! ED!!!!

(Calling out the door.) Bring me something.

> *(Starts closing the door, but then...)*

Candy!

> *(Telephone rings. He goes to answer it.)*

Hello? ...Oh, sorry, Murray. No, just the everyday trials and tribulations of the highborn. What's with you?

*(**ED** bursts through the door in a panic.)*

ED. Arnold! She's here!

ARNOLD. What?

ED. She's here. Headed up the stairs.

ARNOLD. Can't be. It's too early.

ED. There's a woman in the hallway checking all of the apartment numbers.

ARNOLD. What'd she look like?

ED. *(Miming.)* This tall, this wide, carrying a suitcase and a bag of oranges.

ARNOLD. Mayday, Murray, I'll call you back!

> *(**ARNOLD** slams down the phone and begins spinning around the room.)*

ED. Calm down.

ARNOLD. She can't see the place looking like this. She'll walk through the door and head straight for the vacuum cleaner.

> *(**MA** appears in the doorway.)*

MA. I might change my shoes first.

ARNOLD. Ma! Hi! Come on in.

MA. Hello. You must be David.

ED. No. I'm Ed.

MA. How do you do? I'm the mother.

ARNOLD. I really didn't expect you this early.

MA. Obviously.

ED. *(Easing his way to the door.)* Well, I've got to be off. Lovely meeting you, Mrs. Beckoff. I'll be back. Someday.

> *(Out.)*

MA. Nice-looking boy. Who is he?

ARNOLD. That's Ed...

MA. That's enough for now. Let me sit. That bus ride from the airport... I had to stand the whole way. Let me look at you. How do you feel? You look good.

ARNOLD. Good compared to the last time you saw me.

MA. The last time I saw you was at your friend's funeral. You're supposed to look lousy at funerals, it shows respect. You could stand a shave.

ARNOLD. I just got up. Coffee?

MA. Maybe a glass of tea. And a can of Lysol. What am I smelling?

ARNOLD. Ed cooked breakfast.

MA. So we know he's not the cook. What interesting wallpaper.

ARNOLD. It's not wallpaper. I stencilled the design.

MA. Next time use wallpaper. It covers a multitude of sins. Looks nice enough, though why you'd give up that lovely apartment in Brooklyn to move to Manhattan...

ARNOLD. The other place had one bedroom and we needed two.

MA. I thought your roommate's name was David.

ARNOLD. It is.

MA. Three men, two bedrooms... I'll have my tea first.

ARNOLD. Ed's transitory. The sofa's a convertible. Honey?

MA. Lemon. I brought my own Sweet'N Low from the plane. You don't get much light here.

ARNOLD. We get what they call indirect semi-shade. It's good for the plants.

MA. So's manure. How do you find the roaches?

ARNOLD. I turn on the lights.

MA. Arnold, when a man's with his friends he makes wife jokes. When he's with his wife he makes mother jokes. When he's with his mother he lets her make the jokes. You speak to your brother?

ARNOLD. He was over for dinner last week.

MA. He brought a girl?

ARNOLD. Andrea.

MA. He's still seeing her? Any talk of marriage?

ARNOLD. You'll see him tomorrow, you'll ask yourself.

MA. And be accused of meddling?

*(**ARNOLD** comes to the sofa with a tea service all shaped like rabbits.)*

ARNOLD. Ma, you getting shorter?

MA. No. I'm sitting down.

ARNOLD. Why don't we sit in the parlor?

MA. So, who's this Ed?

ARNOLD. A friend.

MA. A friend friend or a euphemism friend?

ARNOLD. He used to be a euphemism, now he's just a friend. So, are you seeing anyone?

MA. Bite your tongue. The only ones who ask me out are old men. And the last thing I need is to become nursemaid to some *alta kaker*.

ARNOLD. You don't meet anyone your own age?

MA. In Miami Beach? Didn't you used to have a friend named Ed who got married?

ARNOLD. Look at that gorgeous tan you've got.

MA. He was a teacher. The girl was too, no? I remember thinking, "Now there's a man with his head on straight." So, what's he doing cooking your breakfast?

ARNOLD. You don't cook for your friends?

MA. Not breakfast.

ARNOLD. He and his wife are separated. He's staying here until he can find a place of his own.

MA. Separated? How come?

ARNOLD. I don't know.

MA. Arnold, the man's staying with you. He must have said something. You're involved?

ARNOLD. No!

MA. Arnold?

ARNOLD. Ma!

MA. You must admit, it sounds a little queer. A man leaves his wife and moves in with his old friend...

ARNOLD. He's spending a few nights on my couch. What's the *magilla*?

MA. No *magilla*. But you'd think he'd stay by friends that have more in common. Y'know, someone he met after the marriage.

ARNOLD. Maybe he needed to get away from all that.

MA. You mean he's still...

(Makes a "gay" motion with her hand.)

ARNOLD. Ma!

MA. What? You don't ask, you don't know. People change.

ARNOLD. No they don't.

MA. What? You think it's so impossible? Believe me, someday you might meet a nice girl...

ARNOLD. Maaaa...

MA. I'm just saying, you never know. Look at your friend Ed.

ARNOLD. He's separated.

MA. Separated. Not divorced. You never know.

ARNOLD. Believe me, Ma, I know.

MA. God doesn't know. My son knows. What's the matter with you? Don't you want children?

ARNOLD. Not the kind you mean.

MA. The kind I mean have arms, legs, a mother, father and chicken pox. How many kinds are there? Arnold, you and your brother are the last of the Beckoffs. Don't you feel you have a duty to continue the family name?

ARNOLD. Not particularly. Anyway, I'm sure my brother will have lots of little Beckoffs running around.

MA. And what if he only has girls?

ARNOLD. I know a surgeon.

MA. I don't get you.

ARNOLD. How about the weather?

MA. I'm glad you reminded me. Your mother. If I didn't have my head screwed on... I brought a couple things from Miami. Look...

(She offers him a tin of cookies.)

MA. I baked you some cookies. Fresh from the sunshiny state.

ARNOLD. David will love these.

MA. I didn't know what to bring. I hadn't seen the place. Go know what you need.

ARNOLD. Oh, you didn't see. Look what I'm making. Beautiful, huh?

> *(He proudly holds up the Afghan throw from the back of the couch. MA greets it with a faint nod.)*

MA. I'm telling you.

ARNOLD. I made this one for out here. I'm going to make one for my bedroom next.

MA. Nice.

ARNOLD. Pretty colors, huh?

MA. Fairy nice.

ARNOLD. *(Winded.)* Maybe you should go unpack while I shower. You can put your things in my room. I got your bag.

MA. Go. I can manage.

ARNOLD. It's the bedroom on the right. Oh, I didn't have time to strip the bed...

MA. Take your shower. I can do it.

ARNOLD. There's fresh linen in the closet.

MA. Go.

ARNOLD. All right. And then we can sit and have a nice long talk.

> *(He slips into the bathroom. MA takes her suitcase and heads for the bedroom.)*

MA. Oy. I'm an old woman who's lived long enough to know there's nothing nice about a long talk.

(A quiet moment onstage. The front door cracks open. DAVID *sticks his head in. Finding the room empty, he enters. He spots the bag of oranges.)*

DAVID. Ah! She has arriven. But where are she?

(Listens at the bathroom door.)

We've got a live one...

*(*ARNOLD *sings in the shower.)*

Wrong one.

*(*DAVID *sneaks along the hallway and disappears. A moment of silence, then a shriek.* DAVID *runs out of the hall pursued by* MA *swinging her purse.)*

MA. A burglar! Arnold, a burglar!

DAVID. I'm not a burglar.

MA. Then what are you – some kind of Peeping Tom who gets his kicks watching middle-aged women strip beds?

DAVID. What would a Peeping Tom be doing in a suit?

MA. How should I know? Maybe you've got a wedding after.

*(*ARNOLD *pops out of the bathroom, dripping in a towel...)*

ARNOLD. David...

MA. This is your roommate?

DAVID. Charmed, I'm sure.

MA. Oh, Arnold, you know that long talk we were going to have? It just got longer.

ARNOLD. David, why aren't you in school?

DAVID. I had a double period of gym but I forgot my uniform. But I told Mr. Kelly about your mother coming and he said I could come home until after lunch. Wasn't that nice of him? Oh, but you gotta call and tell them I wasn't lying.

ARNOLD. So... Ma... This is David.

MA. You're dripping on the floor.

ARNOLD. Hey, I've got an idea. Why don't you go finish unpacking? I'll go finish my shower. And David can set the table for lunch.

DAVID. It's like nine o'clock.

ARNOLD. *(Snapping orders.)* When I tell you to do something I don't want...

> *(Catches **MA** staring.)*

Well, why don't I finish drying off.

MA. You do that.

ARNOLD. So, you'll unpack, right? And you'll set the table, right? And I'll...

MA. Dry up.

ARNOLD. Right.

> *(**ARNOLD** ducks back into the bathroom.)*

DAVID. Would you like a drink?

MA. Maybe later. I'm sorry I hit you.

DAVID. No sweat. I usually charge, but seeing how you're family...

MA. You've got quite a little sense of humor. Would you like to sit down?

DAVID. Sure.

MA. Tell me, David. You go to school?

DAVID. *(Eyeing the cookies.)* Yeah. You make these?

MA. Help yourself. So, you're in college?

DAVID. High school.

MA. High school. How nice. Senior?

DAVID. Freshman.

MA. That's very sweet. Tell me, David, just how old are you?

DAVID. Sixteen... In two months. Something wrong?

MA. Not at all. Sixteen. In two months. You have your whole life ahead of you, while mine is flashing before my eyes. David, it's none of my business, of course, but don't you think you're a little young to be out in the world all alone?

DAVID. No. But the judge did, so here I am.

ARNOLD. *(Sticking his head out.)* Everything all right out here?

MA. Fine dear. Keep drying.

(**ARNOLD** *withdraws.*)

DAVID. You like the place? We cleaned all week for you. Sorry I didn't get back in time to see your face when you got here.

MA. Believe me, that face could not compare to this one.

DAVID. *(Calling out.)* Arnold, come on. You gotta call the school!

MA. Does he make all of your excuses at school?

DAVID. Sure. Who else?

MA. Who else indeed. How about I call the school for you and you can go change your clothes.

DAVID. But I wore this special for you.

MA. I've seen it. It's cute. Now put it away.

DAVID. No, but...

MA. March.

DAVID. Now I see where Arnold gets his technique.

MA. Cute kid.
(Calling to him.) David? Where do you keep the phone numbers?

DAVID. *(Offstage.)* In the phone book.

MA. A little too cute. Arnold, Arnold, what have you gotten yourself into? Here it is, right on top. Must get used a lot. David? What name shall I give them?

DAVID. *(Offstage.)* What?

MA. Who shall I say is being excused? Your last name.

DAVID. *(Reappearing.)* Beckoff, of course.

MA. Now that's a coincidence. Have you and Arnold compared notes to see if there's any family relation?

DAVID. I'm his son. What more relation could there be?

>   (**ARNOLD** *steps out of the bathroom.*)

MA. You're his what?

DAVID. His son.

>   (**ARNOLD** *steps back into the bathroom.*)

Would you like that drink now?

>   (*Blackout.*)

Scene Two

(Later that afternoon.)

(The room is deserted.)

(**ED** *lets himself in with his key.*)

ED. Hello? Anybody here?

ARNOLD. *(Exploding out of the bedroom.)* Where the hell have you been?

ED. Picking up the paper.

ARNOLD. For nine hours?

ED. Why? Did something happen?

ARNOLD. Happen? Happen? What could possibly happen? My mother walked through the door and within three minutes insulted the plane ride, the bus ride, the apartment, Manhattan, my hygiene, Afghan, stencilling and cockroaches. Oh, and she accused me of breaking up your marriage. Okay. So far, so good. So, I go off to take a shower and who makes a surprise appearance but the Patron Saint of Truants himself, Champ David. My mother gets one gander at him and she's all, "So whose little boy are you?" giving the long-awaited cue to my little angel lamb to turncoat 'round and point his every available finger at me.

ED. Oops.

ARNOLD. Oops? Ed, did you say, Oops? No, Ed. Oops is when you fall down an elevator shaft. Oops is mistakenly skinny-dipping with piranha. Oops is when you accidentally douche with Drano. No, Ed, this was no Oops. This was a *(Strangled scream.)*

ED. Cut the dramatics. What happened?

ARNOLD. Nothing happened.

ED. Nothing?

ARNOLD. As in, not a thing. David went to his room. My mother went to my room. And I locked myself in the bathroom making toilet paper flowers and flushing them down the drain. For two hours I flowered and flushed, flowered and flushed. When I finally ran out of paper I came out to find the place deserted.

ED. Well, as the old saying goes, "Leave them alone and they'll come home..."

ARNOLD. ...Dragging a noose behind them. Come help me with dinner.

ED. A quick trip to the men's room first...

> (**ARNOLD** *fetches a plunger from the broom closet and hands it to* **ED.**)

ARNOLD. You'd better take this with you. A thousand sheets really do last longer.

> (*The front door opens and in walk* **MA** *and* **DAVID** *merrily.*)

MA. Arnold, we're home.

ARNOLD. You two were together?

DAVID. I took your mother to school with me.

ED. (*Slipping into the bathroom.*) And you were worried.

ARNOLD. What? Me worry?

DAVID. So, what's for dinner?

MA. You need help? Give me an apron and put me to work.

ARNOLD. No. You're a guest. Ed's going to help.

MA. I wondered what the plunger was for. My feet are screaming for my slippers.

> (*She goes off toward the bedrooms.*)

DAVID. Remember you promised to teach me to chess.

MA. After you do your homework.

DAVID. Homework? She kidding? Arnold? We have a chess set?

ARNOLD. Top shelf of your closet.

> (**DAVID** *goes off.*)

ED. (*Re-entering.*) All fixed.

ARNOLD. From your mouth...

> (**MA** *re-enters wearing a pair of bunny slippers that match* **ARNOLD***'s. She looks*

around the kitchen and finds a bowl of
potatoes.)

MA. So, what're we making? What do you want to do with
these?

ARNOLD. I was just going to bake them. But if you...

MA. You want my latkes?

ARNOLD. I'd love your latkes.

MA. Then you'll get my latkes. You have Matzoh Meal?

ARNOLD. I'll get it.

MA. He has Matzoh Meal. Did I bring him up right?

(**DAVID** *re-enters, taking a book to the couch*
to read.)

ARNOLD. You need eggs?

MA. And an onion.

ED. *(To* **DAVID**.*)* Are you doing homework?

DAVID. No. I'm just reading something for school.

MA. Arnold's father used to love my latkes. But his favorite
was my potato soup. You remember, Arnold?

ARNOLD. I remember, Mama.

MA. It wasn't soup like you'd think. All it was was a
boiled potato with a *bissel* salt and pepper and cream.
Arnold used to call it, Daddy's Potato Water. We were
Depression babies. You understand? You carry that
through your life. The tastes, the smells... They bring
back a cozy feeling of a time you don't quite remember.
You know what I'm talking?

ED. I think so.

MA. Good. Because I don't.

(**ARNOLD** *gives her a kiss.)*

What's that for?

ARNOLD. I'm just glad you're here, Mamala.

MA. Me too, Tatalah.

ED. *(To* **DAVID**.*)* I didn't know you could read.

DAVID. I just look at the pictures.

ED. What is it?

DAVID. Some garbage for English. *(Mispronounces it.) The Ballad of Reading Gaol.*

ED. That's JAIL. Like J-A-I-L.

DAVID. Who am I supposed to believe; you or the book?

ARNOLD. *(Reciting.)* "Yet each man kills the thing he loves,
By each let this be heard
Some do it with a bitter look
Some with a flattering word.
The coward does it with a kiss
The brave man with a sword."

ED. Very good.

ARNOLD. Oscar Wilde. We had to learn it in high school.

ED. Some things never change.

ARNOLD. But they never told us he was gay. They told you, right?

DAVID. I think I would have remembered that.

ARNOLD. You're kidding. That's the whole reason he was sent to jail.

MA. Arnold, could you help me with something here.

ARNOLD. Just a second. Yeah, sure. Ten years earlier Parliament passed laws against being homosexual and Wilde had this young lover...

MA. Arnold, I need a hand.

ED. Anything I could help with?

MA. No, thank you.

ARNOLD. His name was Lord Alfred. And he had this real stick-in-the-mud father who chased them all around the city. Once he even sent a note to Wilde's hotel calling him a sodomite.

MA. Oh, for God's sake, Arnold. Could you change the subject?

    (The room freezes up for a beat.)

ARNOLD. I'll finish later.

    *(**ARNOLD** joins **MA** in the kitchen.)*

ED. Why don't we read it together and I can explain anything you don't understand...

ARNOLD. *(To* **MA.***)* That was very embarrassing.

MA. Excuse me. But what you were telling that boy was very embarrassing.

ARNOLD. I have a responsibility to his education.

MA. I'm sure the people who placed him here did not have that kind of education in mind.

ARNOLD. The people who placed him here had exactly that kind of education in mind and I'll thank you not to interfere.

MA. I am only suggesting you consider the huge responsibility you've taken on. You should be setting an example for the boy.

ARNOLD. And I'm not?

MA. Not when you talk like that you're not. Arnold, you want to live the way you want to live, that's your business. Just wait until the boy's gone. What's a few more months?

ARNOLD. What's a few more months?

MA. What? He's with you on a nine-month program, yes? It's already been six months.

ARNOLD. And what do you think happens then?

MA. He leaves.

DAVID. No, you misunderstood...

> *(***ED*** nudges him hard.)*

Ow. This is getting serious.

ARNOLD. Ma, I don't know what David told you but, after the trial period, if the Court says I can, I will legally adopt David. And believe me, if I have anything to say about it, he's not leaving.

> *(***MA*** tries to say something but is frustrated, angry, and confused. She slams down her apron and storms off to the bedroom.)*
>
> *(Door slam.)*

ARNOLD. THAT was an Oops.

　　(To **DAVID**.*)* What did you say to her?

DAVID. Nothin'.

ARNOLD. Well, you certainly got a way without words. Okay, wish me luck.

DAVID. You going in there?

ARNOLD. I'm taking suggestions.

ED. And don't forget to write.

DAVID. Just remember, we're right in the next room...so talk loud.

ARNOLD. Here goes everything.

　　　　*(***ARNOLD** *exits. A door opens and closes. A beat.* **ED** *and* **DAVID** *rush to the hallway.)*

ED. You hear anything?

DAVID. He waited too long. They're gonna need time to rev up again. Let's eat. You want a sandwich?

　　　　*(***ED** *tries listening in the hall.)*

ED. Could you not holler like that? What was it you told her?

DAVID. What's the difference? Adults only hear what they want.

　　　　(Door slam.)

We're about to get a bullet in.

　　　　*(***MA** *marches into the room and faces a wall.* **ARNOLD** *is close behind, fuming.)*

Anyone care to repose and repast?

ED. *(Grabbing* **DAVID**.*)* Come, Kissinger. I'll teach you to play chess.

DAVID. My sandwich...

ED. You'll concentrate better on an empty stomach.

　　　　*(***ED** *and* **DAVID** *go out toward the bedrooms.)*

ARNOLD. So, is this it? We gonna just stare into space in silence?

MA. You want I should do a Bubble Dance?

ARNOLD. I need a drink.

MA. Arnold, you've done a lot of crazy things in your life, but this...?

ARNOLD. It's not a crazy thing. It's a wonderful thing I'm very proud of.

MA. If you were so proud how come you were too ashamed to tell your mother? Everything else you tell me. You shove your sex life down my throat like aspirin every hour on the hour. But six months he's been here and not a word.

ARNOLD. You're not the easiest person in the world to talk to.

MA. What did I say? Do I tell you how to run your life? No. I learned long ago that no matter what I said you and your brother were going to do just as you pleased anyway. So, I wouldn't say a word. On purpose! You want to know why you didn't tell me? I'll tell you why. Because you knew it was wrong.

ARNOLD. It's not wrong.

MA. Then why?

ARNOLD. I don't know.

MA. You would if you listened.

ARNOLD. Ma, this isn't something we decided to do overnight.

MA. Who we?

ARNOLD. Alan and I.

MA. The two of you were doing this together? Now I've heard everything.

ARNOLD. That's what I love about you. You're so open-minded.

MA. All right. So, Alan's not here. Why's the boy?

ARNOLD. Because with everything else I forgot about the application. Then, one day, the phone rang. They had David for us. I told them about Alan but they said I could probably take David anyway...

MA. And you said, "Send him on over."

ARNOLD. Not at first. But then I thought about it and said yes. I was just so tired of widowing.

MA. Wida-whating?

ARNOLD. Widowing. It's a word of Murray's.

MA. And a nice one at that. What's it supposed to mean?

ARNOLD. You know.

MA. I don't know.

ARNOLD. Widowing. Feeling sorry for yourself. Cursing every time you pass a couple walking hand in hand. Watching tear-jerkers on TV knowing they could only cheer you up. Christ, of everything going on here I never thought that would be the thing I had to explain.

MA. How should I know about whatchamacallit? Did you ever say a word to me?

ARNOLD. I didn't think I had to. It's only been three years since Daddy died.

MA. Wait, wait, wait, wait, wait. Are you trying to compare my marriage with you and Alan? Your father and I were married for thirty-five years, had two children and a wonderful life together. You have the nerve to compare yourself to that?

ARNOLD. I'm talking about the loss.

MA. What loss did you have? You fooled around with some boy. Where do you come to compare that to a marriage of thirty-five years?

ARNOLD. You think it doesn't?

MA. Come on, Arnold. You're not talking to one of your pals.

ARNOLD. I lost someone I loved very much.

MA. So, you felt bad. Maybe you cried a little. What would you know about what I went through? Thirty-five years I lived with that man. He got sick, I brought him to the hospital and you know what they gave me back? I gave them a man, they gave me a paper bag with his watch, wallet and wedding ring. It took me two months until I could get into my bed alone. A year to learn to say

"I" instead of "we." And you're going to compare that to you? How dare you?

ARNOLD. You're right, Ma. How dare I. I couldn't possibly know how it feels to shove someone's clothes in a trash bag and watch garbage men take them away. Or what it feels like to forget and set his place at the table. How about the food that rots in the refrigerator because you forgot how to shop for one? How dare I? Right, Ma? How dare I?

(They both are hollering over one another now...)

ARNOLD.	**MA.**
Listen, Ma, you had it easy. You have all those years to remember. I have five. You had your children and friends to comfort you. I had me. My friends didn't want to hear about it. They said, "What are you griping about? At least you had a lover." And you... You lost your husband in a nice clean hospital. I lost mine out there. They killed him out there on the street. Twenty-three years old, laying dead on the street...	May God strike me dead, whatever I did to my mother to deserve a child speaking to me this way. The disrespect! I only pray that one day you have a child and that he'll open up a mouth to you like the one you opened to me. How dare you talk to me this way?

*(**ARNOLD**'s words penetrate **MA**'s hearing and she stops as he rails on.)*

ARNOLD. ...His head bashed in by a bunch of kids with baseball bats. Killed by children. Children taught by people like you. 'Cause everybody knows that queers don't matter. Queers don't love. And those that do get what they deserve!

*(**MA** flees to the bedroom. Door slams.)*

(**ARNOLD** *catches his breath. He sits.*)

DAVID. *(Sticking his head into the room.)* Wanna keep it down out there? There are people trying to concentrate.

ARNOLD. Sorry.

DAVID. Round one over?

ARNOLD. I didn't mean to say any of that. It all came pouring out. I felt like I was fighting for my life.

DAVID. A duel to the death over little old me.

　　　　(Cuddling.)

I think you're wonderful.

　　　　*(**ED** enters.)*

ARNOLD. Here comes your Tanta Edwina.

ED. All quiet on the west side front?

ARNOLD. We're reloading.

DAVID. Does this mean she's not going to make us dinner?

ARNOLD. Why don't you two go out and get something.

ED. How about you?

ARNOLD. Not hungry.

ED. Let me stay. Maybe we can all talk together.

ARNOLD. Go.

DAVID. Put a candle in the window when it's clear to come home. We'll wait on the bench.

ED. What'll it be? Pizza?

DAVID. You paying?

ED. Sure.

DAVID. Then I know a cozy little bistro...

　　　　*(**ED** and **DAVID** are gone.)*

　　　　*(**ARNOLD** steels himself and...)*

ARNOLD. Round Two. Yoo-hoo. It's safe to come out now. David and Ed have gone out and we have the whole place to fight in.

MA. *(Offstage.)* Enjoy yourself. I'm going to bed.

ARNOLD. Ma, I'm sorry I lost my temper.

MA. *(Offstage.)* I'm glad you're sorry.

ARNOLD. Could you please come out here? We can't talk like this.

MA. *(In the doorway.)* You don't want to talk. You want to fight. But I don't fight with my children. In your life did you ever hear your father and I fight? No. And do you know why? I'll tell you why. Because my whole childhood I listened to fights. My father fought with my mother, my mother fought with me... When I got married I told your father, "Jack, I will talk but I will not fight." And did you ever hear us fight? NO! And now you know why.

ARNOLD. Would you like to sit down?

MA. *(Tentatively comes to couch.)* I'm sitting. And don't holler at me. People say things they don't mean when they holler and you've already said quite enough.

ARNOLD. We won't talk about Alan. Only David.

MA. So, talk.

ARNOLD. Well, why don't you tell me what you already know and we can go on from there.

MA. I don't know anything.

ARNOLD. You spent the day with him. He must have said something.

MA. He's an orphan.

ARNOLD. He's not an orphan.

MA. He said he was an orphan.

ARNOLD. He's not an orphan. They took him away from his parents...

MA. So he's a liar.

ARNOLD. He's not a liar.

MA. Arnold, Arnold... What do you know from raising a child?

ARNOLD. What's to know? Whenever there's a problem I simply imagine what you would do, and do the opposite.

MA. So that's your idea of discussing? To insult me and spit on your father's grave? Arnold, darling, you live

your life the way you want. I put my fist in my mouth,
I don't say a word. But think about that boy. He likes
you. He told me he loves you. He sees you living like
this... Don't you think it's going to affect him?

ARNOLD. Ma... David is gay.

MA. But he's only been here six months.

ARNOLD. He came that way.

MA. No one comes that way.

ARNOLD. What an opening!

MA. By you everything is a joke.

ARNOLD. The whole reason David was placed with me is
so he could grow up with a positive attitude about his
homosexuality.

MA. That's it. I'm finished. The world has gone completely
insane and I'm heading south for the summer.

ARNOLD. You make it very difficult to have an intelligent
conversation.

MA. You want an intelligent conversation? Do what I do –
Talk to yourself! Arnold, you want to live like this? *Gay
gezzinteh hai.* I don't care anymore. You're not going to
put me in my grave like you did your father.

ARNOLD. Now I killed my father?

MA. No! He was thrilled to have a fairy for a son. What
do you think, you walk into a room and say, "Hi Dad,
I'm queer," and that's that? You think that's what we
brought you into the world for? Believe me, if I'd known
I wouldn't have bothered. God should tear out my
tongue, I should talk to my child this way. Arnold, you're
my son, a good person, a sensitive person with a heart,
kennohorrah, like your father. And I try to love you for
that. But you won't let me. You've got to throw me in
the gutter and rub my face in this. You have not spoken
a sentence since I got here without the word Gay in it.

ARNOLD. Because it's who I am.

MA. *(Pointing toward the bedroom.)* If that were all you
could leave it in there where it belongs. No. You're

obsessed with it. You're not happy unless everyone is talking about it. I don't know why you don't just wear a big sign and get it over with.

ARNOLD. Try to imagine the world the other way around. Imagine that every book, every magazine, every TV show and movie told you that you should be homosexual. But you know you're not. And you know that for you this is right...

MA. Stop already. You're talking crazy.

ARNOLD. You want to know what's crazy? After all these years I'm still trying to justify my life.

MA. You call this a life? This is a sickness. But it's what you've chosen for yourself.

ARNOLD. Ma, I'm gay. I don't know why. But that's what I am. For as far back as I can remember. Back before I knew it was even different...

MA. You haven't heard a word I've said.

ARNOLD. *(Exploding.)* I know you'd rather I was straight, but I'm not. Would you also rather I had lied to you? I have friends who'd never dream of telling their parents. Instead they cut their parents out of their lives and they wonder, "Why? Why is my child so distant?" Is that what you'd rather?

MA. It doesn't have to be our every conversation.

ARNOLD. You want to be part of my life? I'm not editing out the things you don't like.

MA. Can we end this conversation?

ARNOLD. No! There's one more thing you'd better understand. I have taught myself to sew, cook, fix plumbing, do taxes... I can even pat myself on the back when necessary.

All so I don't have to ask anyone for anything. There is nothing I need from anyone except for love and respect. And anyone who can't give me those two things has no place in my life. You are my mother. I love you. I do. But if you can't respect me then you have no business being here.

MA. You're throwing me out?

ARNOLD. I'm trying to tell...

MA. Throwing me out. Isn't that nice. Listen, Mister, you get one mother in this world. Only one. Wait. Just you wait.

> (**MA** *heads off to the bedroom, leaving* **ARNOLD.***)*
>
> *(Blackout.)*

Scene Three

(A park bench. Night.)

*(**ED** and **DAVID** enter, just finishing hot dogs.)*

DAVID. How's your hot dog, big spender? Teach you to forget your wallet.

ED. Come on. I've got to walk this off.

DAVID. We're supposed to wait here.
(Pointing.) Our window's right there. This is the bench. This is where it happened. Arnold never brung you here?

ED. No.

DAVID. They were walking back toward the street, Alan and the other guy, when the kids jumped them here. You can see, nowhere to run. There's still a stain on the sidewalk. Well, that's what Arnold says.

ED. He showed you this?

DAVID. Day I moved in. I figured he was trying to scare me from going in the park at night. Figured he was being overprotective, y'know? But I think it's more. No candle in the window yet.

ED. They've got a lot of yelling to catch up on.

DAVID. So, what'd Laurel want with you?

ED. Nothing.

DAVID. Sure.

ED. Really. It was nothing.

DAVID. You don't have to tell me. It's not like we're friends or nothing. What am I to you?

ED. She asked if I was thinking of coming back.

DAVID. That's an easy one. No.

ED. I didn't say that.

DAVID. You won't go back.

ED. Can we change the subject?

DAVID. Sure. Now that you and Laurel are washed up, you gonna sleep around? Just don't put it off too long or you'll wind up like Arnold. He works, eats, sleeps and sticks his nose in my business. That ain't healthy.

ED. You say that like you mean it.

DAVID. Who knows more about sex and its effect on mental health than me? Got any idea how many couches they've laid me out on? Psychiatrically speaking.

ED. Knowing and doing are two different things. You're only fifteen.

DAVID. Someone raised the age of puberty to twenty-one? Kids have sex. Arnold doesn't. Got any suggestions?

ED. None that I'm willing to discuss with a child.

DAVID. I'm not telling you to propose marriage, though I'd be proud to call you Daddy. I'm simply suggesting you could both use a little tension-easing nookie. Sex is very therapeutic.

ED. So, you've said.

DAVID. What do you say?

> (**ARNOLD** *enters, carrying hot dogs like a flower bouquet. He imitates Hepburn in* Stage Door.)

ARNOLD. Hello, Mother. Hello, Dad. The Calla lilies are in bloom again. Such a strange flower. Suitable for any occasion. I carried them on my wedding day and now I place them here in memory of something that has die...

> (*Catches himself.*)

I will never learn when to stop. I brought dinner. I found your wallet upstairs.

ED. Thanks. How'd round two go?

ARNOLD. When I left we both knew who won. Now only Robert Browning does. Ed, would you mind if I spoke to David alone?

ED. Sure.

DAVID. Stay. I want witnesses.

ED. I'll see you upstairs.

> (**ED** *leaves.*)

DAVID. That was a lousy thing to do. He wanted to help.

ARNOLD. I don't need his help. I'm sorry I didn't tell her about you, but it's not because I'm ashamed.

DAVID. And?

ARNOLD. I asked her to leave.

DAVID. You're good at that.

ARNOLD. But whatever happens between my mother and me has nothing to do with us.

DAVID. Don't kid yourself. You're just like her.

ARNOLD. You wouldn't say that if you heard what went on up there.

DAVID. I know what goes on with mothers. You're my fourth. You think it's different because we're both gay, but it's not.

ARNOLD. You're wrong about that.

DAVID. What would you do if I came home with a girl and told you I was straight?

ARNOLD. If you were happy, I'd be happy.

DAVID. Right. You wouldn't worry where you went wrong?

ARNOLD. Not if you were sure it's what you wanted.

DAVID. Then why do you treat Ed like he's lying? The guy keeps trying to tell you how he feels and you call him a closet case.

ARNOLD. See? You don't know what you're talking about. I'd be perfectly happy to believe Ed if just once he thought about the person he was with instead of what sex that person was.

DAVID. You ever meet someone and not know what sex they were?

ARNOLD. That's not what I mean...

DAVID. Shut up and let me finish. I stay with you because I want to. I like living with you. I even like the way you mother me. You make me feel like I've got a home and a bunch of other mushy crap we don't need to get into here. But you can be a real shithead. I'm telling you now – I'm gone if you try to use me as an excuse for sitting home alone or picking a fight with Ed or your mother. You do what you gotta do. I ain't judgin'. But don't blame anybody but yourself, if you get my drift. You get my drift?

(Off **ARNOLD***'s nod.)* I come down too heavy?

>*(***ARNOLD** *shakes his head.)*

Still want me to stay?

(Off another nod.) All right. Now we're dancin'.

ARNOLD. I ever tell you I think you're swell?

DAVID. I got school tomorrow.

ARNOLD. Go on up. I need an airing.

DAVID. Want company?

>*(***ARNOLD** *shakes his head.)*

Okay. See you later.

ARNOLD. David? You're not, are you?

DAVID. What?

ARNOLD. Straight.

>*(***DAVID** *laughs as he walks away.)*

Watch how you cross the street. Stupid kid.

>*(Lights fade to black.)*

Scene Four

(Back in the apartment. Almost dawn.)

(Lights are out. **ED** *is asleep on the open sofa bed. Ma's suitcase sits at the front door.* **ARNOLD** *comes quietly through the front door, weaving a bit. He heads straight for the booze and a glass.)*

ED. *(Waking.)* Huh? What?

ARNOLD. It's me. Go to sleep.

ED. What time is it?

ARNOLD. Five something. Go to sleep.

ED. Wanna talk? You just got home? She said she's leaving.

ARNOLD. I tripped over her bag on my way in.

ED. She didn't want to stay the night but she couldn't get a flight out 'til morning. She was going to spend the night in the airport. I got her calmed down a little.

ARNOLD. Go to sleep.

ED. Stop telling me to go to sleep.

ARNOLD. Fine. Go to hell. Want a drink?

ED. White wine.

(Realizing.)

Nothing, thanks. I saw Laurel today. She told me she's pregnant. She's not.

But she said she was to see if I'd come back if she was. I guess I would've. I don't know. She said she could be if I came back.

(Considers.)

She thinks we're sleeping together. Funny, Laurel and your mother thinking the same thing. Maybe they know something we don't?

*(***ARNOLD*** laughs and sits on the edge of the bed.)*

What's so funny?

ARNOLD. Seems like every time I turn around here we are: Arnold and Ed in bed together.

ED. Talking.

ARNOLD. Talking. Me with a lump in my throat. You with a foot in your mouth.

ED. What'd I say?

ARNOLD. You think I listen?

(Off **ED***'s sad expression.)* Pay me no mind. I'm drunk.

ED. Look, I know I'm not the most sensitive person in the world...

ARNOLD. Ed, take a note: never fish for compliments in polluted waters.

ED. Are you really drunk? Don't think I've ever seen you drunk. Why'd you get drunk?

ARNOLD. *(Knocking on* **ED***'s head.)* Hello? Anybody home?

ED. Care to talk about it?

ARNOLD. Sure. Why should the neighbors have all the fun?

(Lies back onto **ED***'s lap.)*

I had a plan. I thought if I got good and looped I'd get all sentimental and ask my mother to stay. Worked, too, until I saw her sitting in there on the edge of the bed, fully dressed, her Merry Martyr stare burning holes through the door. She thinks I hate her. I know the way her mind works and she thinks I hate her and everything she stands for. And I don't, for the life of me, know how to tell her that what I want more than anything is to have exactly the life she did.

ED. David said you haven't gone out at all since Alan died.

ARNOLD. Let's talk about you.

ED. I can understand not wanting to at first. But you could just go out for a couple of drinks, maybe a quick trip to the backroom.

ARNOLD. You may find this hard to understand but I want more out of life than meeting a pretty face and sitting down on it.

ED. If I made a pass at you now would you let me? It was David's idea. I told him I'd consider it.

ARNOLD. What a pal.

ED. I didn't mean it that way.

ARNOLD. You never do.

ED. This isn't exactly what I want.

ARNOLD. I think the wedding might have given you away.

ED. I didn't want that either. I mean, I did. But...

ARNOLD. I've got some catalogs around here somewhere. You flip through them. When you see what it is you want, give a primal scream and I'll get it for your birthday.

ED. You're not being fair.

ARNOLD. I'm upset, uptight and up to my nipples in Southern Comfort. I'm sorry.

ED. I want another chance with you.

(*Holding* **ARNOLD** *down from escaping.*)

Wait. Think about it. It makes sense. We know each other so well. We know what to expect from each other... Laurel and I together... It wasn't enough. Obviously or I wouldn't be here with you in bed...

ARNOLD. Talking.

ED. Talking. But here. These couple of days with you and David... They've been the closest thing to whatever it is I want. I feel wonderful here.

ARNOLD. "I don't care if the kid ain't mine. I want to be the father of your baby."

ED. I know you're upset about your mother.

ARNOLD. That's not it.

ED. Is it still too soon after Alan?

ARNOLD. God...

ED. I'm asking you to think about it. That's all. Just think.

ARNOLD. How thick could you possibly be? Don't you know that since you called it's all I've thought about?

Last week you walked through that door and ever since I've been playing dutiful wife and mother to your understanding if distant daddy, and David's been having the time of his life playing baby.

ED. It's been wonderful.

ARNOLD. It's a joke. Three grown men playing house.

ED. I love Laurel. Okay, that sounds strange considering the circumstances, but my feelings for her are genuine and just as strong now as the day we got married. But what we have is a friendship not a marriage.

ARNOLD. That's more than most people get.

ED. Arnold, I'm forty. It's time for me to stop jerking around. I want more than a marriage that's at best purposeless, unfulfilling but perfectly comfortable. Whatever you think about us, you can't describe us that way.

ARNOLD. Not the perfect part anyway.

ED. Could you stop making cracks?

ARNOLD. Ed... You think you could bring your friends here? You ready to introduce me to your folks as your lover, and to David as our son? Honey, I just threw my mother – my mother – out of my house and all she wanted to do was not talk about it. You think I'm going to ask less from you?

ED. Isn't it time to find out?

ARNOLD. I don't know. I don't even know what this is supposed to be. I can't look it up in a book or read some *Reader's Digest* article that's going to tell me. All I know is, whatever this is, it's not a grade-B imitation of a heterosexual marriage. I thought Alan and David and I were going to find out together...

ED. How about you me and David find out?

ARNOLD. I can't.

ED. You scared I'm going to walk out again? I can't guarantee anything...

ARNOLD. That's not it.

ED. You know I'd never do anything to hurt David.

ARNOLD. I know that.

ED. What is it Arnold?

ARNOLD. *(From way down deep.)* I'm not Laurel.

ED. I'm counting on that. Are you crying?

ARNOLD. Go home, Ed. You've got a really nice wife who'd do anything for you. She can give you a home, a two-car garage, a child of your own... The whole shebang double-dipped in chocolate and government approved. Go home. I've got nothing like that here.

ED. Your mother did some job on you. Hello? Anybody home? You're going to make me say it, aren't you?

ARNOLD. I don't want you to say anything.

ED. I'll say it. I'm not ashamed. Embarrassed maybe but not ashamed. But I'll be damned if I'm going to say it to your back.

(**ED** *grabs* **ARNOLD** *and pins him to the bed...*)

ED. Are you ready?

ARNOLD. You're going to wake my mother.

ED. Let her hear. I hope they're both listening. Might as well let everyone know... Arnold Beckoff, I love...

(**DAVID** *enters, interrupting.*)

DAVID. What's going on in here? Something interesting, I hope.

ARNOLD. Why are you up? And dressed?

DAVID. My alarm went off ten minutes ago. So, is this a closed marriage or can anyone jump in?

(**DAVID** *dives into bed between the two. His black eye is now visible.*)

ARNOLD. And baby makes three. Any news from the war front?

DAVID. I heard shuffling.

ARNOLD. I'd better prepare for the grand exit. Give me a boost, I think my battery's dead.

　　　　(**DAVID** *pushes* **ARNOLD** *to an upright position.*)

Please, no one get up.

　　　　(**ARNOLD** *exits to the bathroom.*)

DAVID. So?

ED. Struck out. He said no.

DAVID. So what? Arnold always says no first and then thinks about it. Watch.
(*Calling out.*) Arnold? Want breakfast?

ARNOLD. (*Offstage.*) No, thanks.

DAVID. Five – four – three – two…

ARNOLD. (*Offstage.*) David? Maybe I'll have a egg.

DAVID. Most contrary person I know.

ED. We'd better get dressed.

DAVID. I am dressed.

ED. (*Heading off.*) Then start coffee.

DAVID. Sure thing. As soon as I care.

　　　　(**DAVID** *switches on the radio…*)

RADIO. …Plaza 6-6654 with your requests. It's six fifty-four and I'm here with you, dedicated to the one you love. And now an oldie by request from Beulah to Robert and Michael. Guess that gal can't make up her mind. All right, Beulah, here it is…

ARNOLD. (*Coming from the bathroom.*) What are you listening to?

DAVID. Want me to change it?

ARNOLD. No. I ever tell you about the time Alan dedicated a song to me on the radio? Of course they got it wrong, "To Arnold from Ellen." Still, it was very romantic.

DAVID. Is your mother staying for breakfast?

ARNOLD. Ask her. She shown her face yet?

DAVID. Nope.

ARNOLD. Go see if she needs some help.

> (**DAVID** *starts off to the bedroom.*)

DAVID. "Into the jaws of death, Into the mouth of Hell."

> (*A moment of peace and then* **MA** *appears, dragging* **DAVID** *behind her.*)

MA. Arnold, did you see this eye? Come. Let me put ice on it.

DAVID. I'm all right.

ARNOLD. Ma, he's had it for two days. He covered it with makeup yesterday for you.

DAVID. I'm okay. Really. But thanks.

> (**ED** *re-enters.*)

ED. Come on, Champ. I'll take you out for breakfast.

DAVID. (*Suddenly has an idea.*) Great. Just gotta do something first.

> (**DAVID** *goes off to the bedroom.* **ED** *approaches* **MA.**)

ED. It was a pleasure meeting you, Mrs. Beckoff.

MA. The pleasure was mine. I hope you and your wife come to your senses. Couples should learn to live with conflict. After all, a problem is never as permanent as a solution.

ED. Thank you.

(*Calling out.*) David?

> (**ARNOLD** *signals* **ED** *to join him off on the side.*)

ARNOLD. Ed... What we were talking about before... I don't know. We can talk.

ED. That's all I'm asking. Good. Good.

DAVID. (*Re-entering with a grin.*) All done. Let's go.

MA. You take care of that eye.

DAVID. Thanks.

(To **ED**.*)* Remember your wallet this time? What's wrong with you? You look like somebody kicked you in the head.

> (**ED** *pushes* **DAVID** *out the door. They are gone, but not before* **ED** *lets out a loud, celebratory "Yahoo!")*

ARNOLD. He likes the wallpaper in the hall. Covers a multitude of sins.

MA. I should be going myself.

ARNOLD. Ma, you can stay...

MA. With your brother? No. I'll call him from home and tell him I changed my plans.

ARNOLD. I'm going to tell him what happened.

MA. What else do you want to do to me, Arnold? What? You want to turn my son against me? Go ahead. You want me to leave? I'm leaving. You want me to change? I'm too old. I can't. I can't, I can't, I can't. So, you do what you have to do, and I'll do what I have to do, and I hope you're satisfied. Believe me, if I had ever opened a mouth to my mother like you did to me you'd be talking to a woman with a size-six wedgie sticking out of her forehead. But I didn't raise my children like that. I wanted to earn their respect. Not because I beat it into them. Go know!

ARNOLD. We're going to start all over again?

MA. Yes! Because you can't put all the blame on me. It's not fair. You think I didn't know about you, Arnold? Believe me, I knew. I knew and I said, no. I hoped... What's the difference? I knew and I turned my back. But I wasn't the only one. There were things you should have told me. You opened a mouth to me about Alan. How was I supposed to know?

ARNOLD. So you could have said what? Told me he's better off dead?

MA. Or maybe I could have comforted you. Told you what to expect. But you cheated me out of your life and then blamed me for not being there.

> (*She turns and goes to the door. She picks up her suitcase and then stops...*)
>
> (*Back still to* **ARNOLD**.)

About this Ed. You love him?

ARNOLD. I don't know. I think so.

MA. Like you loved Alan?

ARNOLD. No. They're very different. Anyway, it's easier to love someone who's dead. They make so few mistakes. Mama, I miss him.

> (**MA** *puts down the suitcase and takes a small step toward her son.*)

MA. Give yourself time. It gets better. But, Arnold, it doesn't ever go away. You can work longer hours, adopt a son, fight with me... Whatever. It'll still be there. But that's all right. It becomes a part of you like wearing a ring or pair of glasses. You get used to it. And it's good. It's good because it makes sure you don't forget. You don't want to forget him, do you? So, it's good.

> (*Telephone rings.*)

Go. Answer it. It might be something with that son of yours.

> (*They exchange a knowing glance.* **ARNOLD** *answers the phone.*)

ARNOLD. Hello? ...Oh, hi, Murray... What? The radio is on... All right. I'm turning.

> (*He hangs up the phone and goes to the radio.*)

It's Murray. Something's on the radio. I don't know.

(**ARNOLD** *turns up the radio and listens.*)

RADIO. ...No. I just checked with my producer who took the call. I had it right. So, here it is, a dedication from David to Arnold with all his love.

["I Will Never Turn My Back on You" by Big Maybelle.]*

(**ARNOLD** *stares at the radio.* **MA** *slips quietly out the door with her suitcase.*)

ARNOLD. You hear that, Ma? Stupid kid. Ma, you...

(**ARNOLD** *turns and sees the room is empty. He runs to the bedroom. He checks the bathroom. He runs out the front door. No Ma.*)

(*He shuts the door behind him and takes in the empty room.*)

(*Picking up a photo of Alan, he takes it to the sofa and sits. He finds David's book there and, of course, Ed's wallet is right on the side. And then he sees the tin of cookies from Ma.*)

(*He gathers all of these things into his chest dearly.*)

(*The music builds.*)

(*The lights fade.*)

End of Play

---

*A license to produce *Torch Song* does not include a performance license for "I Will Never Turn My Back on You." The publisher and author suggest that the licensee contact ASCAP or BMI to ascertain the music publisher and contact such music publisher to license or acquire permission for performance of the song. If a license or permission is unattainable for "I Will Never Turn My Back on You," the licensee may not use the song in *Torch Song* but should create an original composition in a similar style or use a similar song in the public domain. For further information, please see Music Use Note on page 3.